CATHOLIC HIGH SCHOOLS AND MINORITY STUDENTS

CATHOLIC HIGH SCHOOLS

AND MINORITY STUDENTS

Andrew M. Greeley

Transaction Books
New Brunswick (U.S.A.) and London (U.K.)

Library of Congress Catalog Number: 81-23131
ISBN: 0-87855-452-1 (cloth)
Printed in the United States of America

Library of Congress Cataloging in Publication Data
Greeley, Andrew M., 1928-
  Catholic high schools and minority students.
  1. Catholic high schools—United States. 2. Minorities—Education
(Secondary)—United States. 3. Educational surveys—United States.
I. Title.
LC501.G73   377'.82   81-23131
ISBN 0-87855-452-1   AACR2

Contents

123109

List of Tables

Acknowledgments

The data analyzed in this book were collected by the National Opinion Research Center under contract with the National Center for Education Statistics. The analysis was funded by grants from the Ford Foundation and the Spencer Foundation. I am grateful to the members of the High School and Beyond team for their cooperation, especially to James Coleman, Carol Stocking, Fansayde Calloway, and Lawrence Dornacker. Comments from other NORC colleagues were very helpful—Robert Michael, Norman Bradburn, William Mc-Cready. Data processing assistance at NORC was provided by Donald Tom, and typing by Mary Kotecki and Chris Lonn. University of Arizona assistance was available from Michael Hout and Dolores Vura of the Department of Sociology, and Daniel Bailey of the Computer Center.

1.

The Problem

The High School and Beyond (HS&B) study is a nationally representative sample survey of 1980 high school sophomores and seniors in the United States. As a large-scale, longitudinal survey, the study's primary purpose is to observe the educational and occupational plans and activities of young people as they pass through the American educational system and take on their adult roles. The study should ultimately contribute to an understanding of student development and of the factors that determine individual education and career outcomes. Such information is useful as a basis for review and reformulation of federal, state, and local policies affecting the transition of youth from school to adult life.

The availability of this longitudinal data base encourages in-depth research for meeting the educational policy needs of the 1980s at local, state, and federal levels. HS&B data should contribute to evaluating: the strength of secondary school curricula; the demand for postsecondary education; problems of financing postsecondary education; the adequacy of postsecondary alternatives open to high school students; the need for new types of educational programs and facilities to develop the talents of our youth; and the relationships between the educational, vocational, and personal development of young people and the institutional, familial, social, and cultural factors affecting that development.

HS&B is the second in a program of longitudinal studies sponsored

1

by the National Center for Education Statistics. This study is similar to NCES's first, the National Longitudinal Study of the High School Class of 1972 (NLS-72), which began in 1972 and has completed its fourth followup survey. NCES's longitudinal studies program is based on the assumption that federal, state, and local policies affecting the transition from school to work ought to be grounded on factual analyses of intervening processes of the American educational system, not simply on the inputs and diplomas awarded. The longitudinal studies program provides statistics on the education, work, and family experiences of young adults during the pivotal years during and immediately following high school. The Fourth Followup of the NLS-72 provides current information on the outcomes of schooling seven years after high school, while the base-year HS&B study provides current information on high school experiences, near the beginning of the transition to adult life.

The HS&B study design seeks to gather the same type of data collected by NCES's first longitudinal study. The study of the HS&B senior cohort replicates many aspects of the NLS-72, both in the questionnaires and in the cognitive tests, so interstudy comparisons can be made of economic and social changes occurred in the eight years since 1972. The second study differs from the first in two significant ways. First, it addresses elements in the educational process that were ignored in the first study. HS&B is the first longitudinal study of students to survey parents concerning their aspirations for their children and their ability and desire to pay for the fulfillment of these aspirations. HS&B is also the first study to survey teachers concerning their assessment of their students' futures. Second, it extends the scope of the population to the sophomores of 1980 as well as the seniors, and thus makes possible a fuller understanding of the dimensions of secondary school experience, its long-term impact on students, and the factors that influence the process of dropping out of school early.

The base-year survey was conducted in spring 1980. The study design included a highly stratified national probability sample of over 1,100 high schools with 36 seniors and 36 sophomores per school. (In those schools with fewer than 36 seniors or sophomores, all eligible students were included in the sample.) Cooperation from both schools and students was excellent. Over 30,000 sophomores and 28,000 seniors enrolled in 1,015 public and private high schools across the nation participated in the base-year survey.[1] The samples represent the nation's 10th- and 12th-grade populations, totaling about 3,800,000 sophomores and 3,000,000 seniors in more than 21,000 schools in spring 1980.

Questionnaires and cognitive tests were administered to each student in the HS&B sample. The student questionnaire covered school experiences, activities, attitudes, plans, selected background characteristics, and language proficiency. Other groups of respondents provided other types of information. The administrator in each selected school filled out a questionnaire about the school; teachers in each school were asked to make comments on students in the sample; twins in the sample were identified and their counterpart twins were also surveyed; and a sample of parents of sophomores and seniors (about 3,600 for each cohort) was surveyed primarily for information on financing of higher education. The total survey effort thus provided a comprehensive data base for analyses in education and other areas of social sciences.

This study focuses on a single subject—minority students attending Catholic secondary schools—and addresses a single problem which will give structure and shape to the present volume: Why black and Hispanic students who attend Roman Catholic secondary schools display much higher levels of academic effort and achievement than black and Hispanic young people attending public schools.

The nature of the problem is clear from Table 1.1. On an academic performance index (composed of reading and math scores), the Hispanic students in Catholic schools are approximately half a standard deviation higher than their public school counterparts. They are a standard deviation less likely to report discipline problems, they are twice as likely to do five or more hours of homework a week, and almost 30 percentage points more likely to say they expect to graduate from college.

In this report, we will search for an explanation of these dramatic educational phenomena. We will seek an answer to the problem (Table 1.2) first of all in the family characteristics of the student, then in his own characteristics, and finally in certain school characteristics.

It may be assumed on the basis of vast literature on educational research that outcome is largely the result of input and that therefore the income, education, and college aspirations of a student's parents, the learning environment in the family, and parental monitoring of his/her homework might account for most if not all differences in outcome. In addition, the young person's psychological well-being, his

TABLE 1.1
The Problem of the Catholic High School and Minority Students

	Catholic	Public
A) ACADEMIC PERFORMANCE INDEX Z Score (Percent of standard deviation from the mean)		
White	25	-01
Black	-44	-91
Hispanic	-23	-77
B) SCHOOL DISCIPLINE INDEX Z Score High score = low problem)		
White	43	-49
Black	32	-50
Hispanic	58	-58
C) HOMEWORK (Percent doing more than 5 hours of homework a week)		
White	42	23
Black	44	22
Hispanic	44	22
D) COLLEGE ASPIRATIONS (Percent expect to graduate from college)		
White	64	42
Black	77	48
Hispanic	66	38

aspirations for college, the way he uses his time, and his addiction to television might all be properly considered background characteristics and might well account for whatever differences remain between public and Catholic school students who are black and Hispanic.

If differences remain after these ten background variables are taken into account, we will seek an explanation in characteristics of the

TABLE 1.2
Model to Explain Differences in Standardized Achievement Test Scores

FAMILY CHARACTERISTICS

    FATHER ABSENT

    Income

    Parental education

    Parental aspirations for student's college attendance

    Family learning environment (specific place to study, daily news-
    paper, encyclopedia, typewriter, more than 50 books, a room of
    one's own, pocket calculator)

    Family monitoring of homework

STUDENT CHARACTERISTICS

    Psychological well-being

    College aspirations in Grade 8

    Hours of TV watched per week

    Use of time (high on reading for pleasure, reading the newspaper,
    talking with mother or father about personal experiences, low on
    visiting with friends at local gathering place, going out on
    dates, driving around, talking with friends on telephone, thinking
    or daydreaming alone)

SCHOOL CHARACTERISTICS

    Owned by a religious order

    Student rating of teachers (quality of instruction and interest in
    students)

    Discipline problems (truancy, skip class, talk back to teacher,
    refuse to obey instructions, get in fights with each other,
    attack or threaten teachers)

school—its ownership by a religious order (assuming that the strong internal community ties religious order may facilitate academic development), the absence of disciplinary problems in the school, and the student's rating of the quality of academic instruction.

To briefly anticipate the findings of this report, the expectations of young people that they will graduate from college is almost entirely the result of background characteristics—familial and personal. Our model is able to account for some disciplinary differences between Catholic and public schools (two-thirds of the difference), but unexplained differences remain. Finally, after all background characteristics are taken into account and even disciplinary atmosphere of the schools is held constant, the quality of classroom instruction makes a substantial contribution both to the higher achievement scores and the propensity to do more homework of black and Hispanic young people attending Catholic high schools.

The data examined in this project were collected in NORC's High School and Beyond project carried out under contract to the National Center for Education Statistics. In the data collection, Catholic schools with more than 30 percent black or Hispanic enrollment were oversampled, so a little more than 7,000 Catholic school students were included in the sample, approximately 2,000 of them minority group members. The principal analysis in this report was done with a data file containing information on all the Catholic school students and 7,000 randomly sampled public school students.

Questionnaires were also administered to the principals of the high schools from which are taken the data analyzed in chapter 9, as well as the religious order ownership item used in previous chapters.

With samples this size, virtually all differences are statistically significant, and the only attention paid to questions of statistical significance in the present report will be when after analytic models have been used, the remaining differences between public and Catholic school minority students are not statistically significant.

In most of the analysis in this book, a technique of dummy variable multiregression analysis will be used that is especially well suited for comparing two groups. The illustration in Table 1.3 demonstrates how the method works.

In the first step, the dependent variable (in the illustration, political activism) is entered into a regression equation with a dummy variable representing the two groups being studied (in the table, Jews receive a score of 1 and non-Jews, in this case Italians, receive a score of 0). The B in the output from the regression equation represents the difference between the two groups. The scale used has been standardized so that the mean is 0 and the standard deviation is 1, then the B represents a standardized (or Z) score—the proportion of the standard deviation that separates the mean score of one group from the mean score of the

TABLE 1.3
Fictional Illustration of Dummy Variable Regression as a Method of
Comparing and Explaining the Different Mean Scores of Two Groups

Political activism
Z Score
(Percent of a standard deviation)

Jewish more active than Italians

Raw difference	50
Parental political activism	35
"Authoritarianism" of family of origin	30
Educational attainment	08[*]

[*]Difference not significant

other. In the illustrative table, Jews are half a standard deviation higher than Italians on the scale of political activism; a Z score of 50 means 50 percent of a standard deviation separates the scores of the two groups.

In subsequent regression equations, new explanatory variables are entered in an order previously specified by theory. Thus, in the illustrative equation, the first possibility to consider is that Italians are less active politically than Jews because their parents were less active. The decline of the Z score from 50 to 35 indicates that a little more than a third of the difference between Italians and Jews can be accounted for by parental activism. In the next step of the model, the family structure of Italian families (more authoritarian) is added to the model *in addition to parental activism*. The difference between the two groups declines from 35 to 30 showing that family structure makes a contribution to explain the difference between Jews and Italians but it is not as important as family political example. Finally, if educational attainment is added to the previous explanatory variables, the difference between the two groups diminishes to 8 percent of the standard deviation and becomes insignificant. One would therefore interpret the model presented in the table as indicating that most of the difference between Italians and Jews in political activism can be accounted for by different levels of educational attainment and different levels of parental activism, and that while the somewhat more authoritarian structure of the Italian family does make a contribution to the difference, it is the least important of the three explanations.

This (entirely fictional) model illustrates the technique used in this book in accounting for differences. The researcher can not only test the capacity of this theory to explain the differences observed, he can also see the relative contribution of each level of explanation. But he must specify the order in which the variables are to be entered. In the analysis in this book, we assume a conservative approach to the question of school impact: we tilt in the direction of the input explanation in an attempt to minimize the potential impact of the school itself and particularly of the quality of educational instruction in the school so that the analytic bias is toward a background explanation of the differences presented in Table 1.1. It is possible that a high achievement score will affect the college aspirations of the person and that the quality of academic instruction will have an effect on how the student uses his time and the amount of hours he watches TV each week. Nonetheless, because of the conservative bias we have assumed for methodological reasons in this report, it is presumed that academic aspirations and the use of time and even the disciplinary atmosphere of the school are primary in their impact on the quality of educational instruction; background characteristics are entered before school characteristics and the disciplinary characteristics of the school are entered into the model before the instructional characteristics. The reason for such a conservative tilt is to heighten the probability (and in research one deals with probabilities, not with certainties) that the effect that we finally attribute to the quality of instruction in the school is not the effect of some background variable that ought to have been taken into account first (Table 1.2).

There is virtually no literature on the effect of Catholic secondary education, to say nothing of a literature on the effect of such education on minority students. One has the impression, however, from conversations and discussions, that most educators are willing to concede that the private, often "college-preparatory" Catholic secondary schools would be more successful with the students who entered them. Again one has the impression that most educators would attribute this effect to the background characteristics of the student whose family decided to enroll him in Catholic school and in the Catholic school's special ability to deal with disciplinary problems. The conventional wisdom of educators tilts in the direction of an "input" explanation for such successes of private secondary schools. The report is methodologically biased in the direction of such an explanation. However, in some measures of educational outcome there seems to be a residual Catholic school effect which can be attributed to the quality of instruction. This does not conclusively settle the issue, but it does tilt the assumption away from an "input" explanation and in the direction of a "school effect" explanation. Minimally any further research done on Catholic education and minority students must seek not only to develop ever more refined measures of background characteristics, but also measures which will enable investigators to examine more closely the impact of Catholic secondary schools on minority students and especially the reasons why these students are so much likelier than students in public schools to rate the quality of academic instruction as "excellent."

James Coleman and his colleagues[2] have prepared an overall description of differences between public and nonpublic schools observed in the High School and Beyond project. The present volume will not repeat except in brief summary any of the material to be found in that work. Approximately 6 percent of secondary students in the United States are enrolled in Catholic schools (12 percent in Rhode Island, 11 percent in Pennsylvania, 10 percent in New York, 14 percent in the District of Columbia, 11 percent in Delaware, 10 percent in Louisiana, 10 percent in Illinois, and 10 percent in Nebraska), 15 percent of the sophomores and 14 percent of the seniors in Catholic schools are either black or Hispanic—approximately 6 percent black and 8 or 9 percent Hispanic.[3]

Whether Catholic schools are more or less integrated than public schools is a complex question.[4] Since a lower percentage of students attending public schools are white (approximately 80 percent), students attending those public schools have a somewhat higher index of interracial and interethnic contact.[5] Seven percent of the schoolmates of the average white student in the public school will be black as opposed to 4 percent of the average white student whose schoolmates will be black in the Catholic school. On the other hand, 38 percent of the average black schoolmates will be white if he attends a public school and 58 percent will be white if he attends a Catholic school. The index of segregation (the proportion of students within a school "system" who would have to be moved in order to achieve perfect integration) is .49 for public schools and .32 for Catholic schools.

Similarly, 5 percent of the average white students will have Hispanic schoolmates whether he/she goes to a public or Catholic school, but 52 percent of Hispanics in public schools and 63 percent of those in Catholic schools will have white schoolmates and the segregation index of Hispanics and whites is .30 in public schools and .25 in Catholic schools. Given the proportion of blacks, whites, and Hispanics in the respective "systems," Catholic schools are somewhat less ethnically and racially segregated than public schools (on a national average), and a black or Hispanic who attends Catholic school is more likely to have white schoolmates than a black or Hispanic who attends public secondary schools.

Similarly, low-income students are somewhat more likely to attend school with high-income classmates if they go to Catholic school, though only 6 percent of the average high-income students' schoolmates will be from low-income families if he/she attends a Catholic school and 12 percent will be from low-income families if he/she attends public school.

Little evidence then can be found that Catholic schools are "rich men's segregated enclaves," as they were called during the controversy over tuition tax credits. Minimally it must be said that a black or Hispanic attending a Catholic school is more likely to have white schoolmates, and a poor person attending Catholic school is more likely to have affluent schoolmates than if he/she were going to a public school. An affluent or white young person attending Catholic school will have nonwhite or poor classmates in proportions not greatly different from what would have obtained if he/she had gone to a public school. Catholic schools then are sufficiently integrated racially and ethnically.[6]

There is little difference between young men and young women in their academic performance scores as these are used in the present project, and therefore, with one or two exceptions, no attention will be paid in this report to sexual differentiation, though a later project is planned in which the effect of Catholic secondary education on the self-image of women will be considered.

Chapter 2 will consider background characteristics of the family and the student which might explain the different outcomes of Catholic and public schools for black and Hispanic students. Chapter 3 will discuss disciplinary differences between the two kinds of schools, and chapter 4 will be devoted to a discussion of the different academic outcomes. After a brief overview of some of the religious results of Catholic education in chapter 5, chapter 6 will provide some solutions to the problems portrayed in Table 1.1. Chapter 7 will investigate the interrelationship between Catholic schools, social class, and academic outcome, and chapter 8 will also consider the effect of academic tracking in Catholic and public schools on educational outcome. Chapter 9 will offer some material on the finances of Catholic secondary education, and chapter 10 will summarize the report, make suggestions for further research, and offer some tentative policy conclusions.

NOTES

The materials in the first six paragraphs are based on the NORC capsule summary of the High School and Beyond research. Full details as well as a codebook are available from the National Center for Education Statistics under the title, "High School and Beyond Information for Users, Base Year (1980) Data."

1. The overall response rate for schools was 91 percent and for students was 84 percent.
2. James Coleman, Thomas Hoffer, and Sally Kilgore, "Public and Non-Public Schools," report for the National Center for Education Statistics, September 2, 1980, preliminary draft, National Opinion Research Center.
3. Half of the black students in Catholic high schools are not Catholic. More than nine-tenths of the white and Hispanic students are Catholic (92 percent of the white and 96 percent of the Hispanic). Ninety-five out of 100 Catholic secondary schools accept non-Catholic students.
4. Minority students in Catholic high schools represent about 1 percent of the secondary school students in the country—a little more than 5 percent of all the minority secondary school students in the country.
5. See Coleman et al., p. 2.6.
6. The term *racial and ethnic* is used to cope with the problem that the minorities are in one case racial and in the other case ethnic or linguistic. No distinction is possible in the present research between Cuban, Puerto Rican, and Mexican Hispanics. The interested reader is referred to a work by Francois Nielsen on the Hispanic student in the High School and Beyond study.

2.

Demography and Aspirations

To choose a private high school for one's child is to exercise an option. Similarly for a child to accept such a choice is also an exercise of an option (and is not altogether impossible the child may initiate the decision to attend a private high school). It is not, however, a common option, since more than 90 percent of the secondary students in the country do not go to such schools. Moreover, it is not an inexpensive option. Catholic secondary school probably costs the families patronizing them more than a thousand dollars a year (per child) when the cost of books is taken into account. It is therefore altogether reasonable to assume that those who choose to exercise the option are systematically different from those who do not make such a choice. In all likelihood such families are both more affluent and more concerned about education than are the families of those who attend public schools. It may well be that the differences in outcome of minority young people attending Catholic schools is the function of their different family background.

Such an explanation cannot be completely excluded even when one holds constant a dozen or so background variables. One may not have eliminated some critical family effect which accounts for the different educational outcomes. All one can do by holding constant background variables is diminish the probability that a background explanation is sufficient, either one that emphasizes family characteristics, those of

13

the individual student, or some combination of both. The probability that one has uncovered an authentic school effect is enhanced if something in the environment of the school which is unlikely to be connected with family background does account for the differences remaining even after background characteristics have been held constant. But it is the nature of the logic of social research that it can only diminish probability of a given explanation, not eliminate it completely.

In this chapter we will investigate the demographic, economic, and environmental differences among young people who attend Catholic schools and those who attend public schools. The differences are considerable. It would be most unlikely that they do not have an effect on the educational outcome. The question to be addressed in subsequent chapters is whether other dynamics have to be considered in addition to background characteristics.

ECONOMIC AND DEMOGRAPHIC DIFFERENCES

Catholic school students are less likely to come from father-absent families (Table 2.1), though the biggest difference (8 percentage points) is to be found among whites attending Catholic school. While 50 percent of blacks attending public schools are from father-absent families, so too are 45 percent of those attending Catholic schools (28 percent and 23 percent respectively for Hispanic students). A father-absent family is characteristic of many black students in both kinds of educational institutions and suggests that for those attending Catholic schools from such families there is a special economic sacrifice involved for the mother.

Catholic school secondary students are also more likely to come from grandparent-present families (Table 2.2)—twice as likely in the case of Hispanics (7 percent versus 15 percent). Whether the extended family as represented by a grandparent present could be expected to facilitate or impede educational attainment is not clear. In the present research there was no significant correlation between the presence of grandparents and educational outcome and this variable was dropped from the analysis.

It is generally believed—with considerable evidence—that the larger the family, the less likely its members are to achieve, in all likelihood because each of them is able to receive less individual attention from

TABLE 2.1
Father-Absent Family
(Percent)

	Public	Catholic
White	21	13
Black	50	45
Hispanic.	28	23

parents. One might expect Catholics in parochial schools to have somewhat larger families because they might be more religiously devout. One might expect the opposite in black and Hispanic families because the smaller the family, the more resources the family might have available for providing private education for its children. Such seems to be the case, though the size of the Catholic school Catholic family is only slightly larger than that of the public school Catholic family. However, Catholic school black and Hispanic families are much smaller than their public school counterparts. As we shall see in a subsequent chapter, the negative correlation between family size and achievement is relatively small and is eliminated from the model by far more powerful predictor variables.

Catholic school secondary students come from much more affluent families (Table 2.4); 42 percent of whites (as opposed to 29 percent of the public school whites), 28 percent of blacks, and 24 percent of Hispanics (as opposed to 11 percent of public school minorities) report

TABLE 2.2
Grandparent-Present Family
(Percent)

	Public	Catholic
White	5	7
Black	7	9
Hispanic.	7	15

TABLE 2.3
Number of Children in Family
(in Addition to Respondent)

	Public	Catholic
White	2.9	3.1
Black	4.3	2.9
Hispanic.	4.3	2.7

more than $25,000 a year in family income. Black and Hispanic Catholic school students are not as affluent as white Catholic school students, but they are far more affluent than their minority counterparts in public schools and their parents (Table 2.5) are much more likely to have attended college. Approximately two-fifths of the Catholic school respondents reported college-educated mother or father as opposed to less than one-fifth of the public school blacks and less than a quarter of the Hispanic public school students. Blacks who attend Catholic schools are 8 percentage points (41 percent versus 33 percent) more likely to have a college-educated mother than a white Catholic school attender. Since educational outcome is heavily influenced by the social status of the family, one must expect inevitably that some, not all, of the Catholic school effect would be the result that the young people who attend such schools (be they white or black) come from more affluent and better-educated families.

TABLE 2.4
Income by Race and School Type
(Percent over $25,000)

	Public	Catholic
White	29	42
Black	11	28
Hispanic.	11	24

TABLE 2.5
Mother and Father's Education
(Percent Attended College)

	White		Black		Hispanic	
	Public	Catholic	Public	Catholic	Public	Catholic
Mother .	24	33	18	41	11	25
Father .	32	48	17	38	17	27

Their fathers are also much more likely to be owners or professionals; 15 percent for Catholic school blacks versus 6 percent for public school blacks (Table 2.6), and 24 percent for Catholic school Hispanics versus 8 percent for public school Hispanics. Their mothers are also more likely to be professionals or proprietors; 20 percent of the blacks in Catholic schools versus 11 percent of those in public schools and 10 percent of Hispanics in Catholic schools versus 6 percent in public schools. Blacks in Catholic schools are twice as likely to say that their mothers are school teachers as those in public schools (most of these women are probably teaching in public schools), and also twice as likely to have fathers who are in "protective services"— work for the police or the fire department. It would appear then that members of the public service bureaucracy are especially likely to seek out Catholic schools for their children.

Whites who attend Catholic schools (Table 2.8) are marginally more likely to have an immigrant background and blacks who attend Catholic schools marginally less likely. Hispanics who attend Catholic schools are 30 percentage points more likely to say that their father and/or mother were immigrants. One presumes that most of them are Cuban-American rather than Mexican-American families, and the pattern of academic achievement scores (Table 2.9) of Hispanics when one takes into account father's education and immigrant status is quite interesting. Catholic schools seem to have their most notable impact (64 standardized points) on those who have college-educated immigrant fathers and on those whose fathers did not immigrate nor attend college (48 standardized points). They have less effect on immigrants whose fathers did not attend college and on those whose native-born fathers did attend college. One may speculate that the first group in Table 2.9 is largely Cuban and the last group largely native-born

TABLE 2.6
Father's Occupation by Race and Religion
(Percent)

	White		Black		Hispanic	
	Cath.	Non-Cath.	Cath.	Non-Cath.	Cath.	Non-Cath.
Not living with father	5.8	8.3	23.4	21.4	11.1	12.6
Clerical	2.7	1.4	3.0	3.0	2.2	3.4
Craftsman	12.4	14.1	9.0	11.5	14.8	17.0
Farmer, Farm Manager	.6	4.8	.0	2.5	.5	6.1
Homemaker	.0	.1	.3	1.2	.2	1.0
Laborer	6.2	7.4	8.0	10.7	6.4	11.6
Manager, Admin.	16.4	12.2	9.0	6.0	8.9	6.5
Military	.0	1.8	1.7	3.5	1.0	1.0
Operative	6.1	11.4	8.4	14.2	10.1	10.9
Prof. 1	10.2	5.2	7.0	2.2	8.1	3.1
Prof. 2, Advanced	7.3	4.2	3.7	1.5	6.4	.0
Proprietor, Owner	7.6	7.7	4.3	2.5	9.1	5.1
Protective Service	4.4	2.6	4.0	1.5	1.2	2.0
Sales	6.7	3.5	2.0	.5	3.2	2.4
School Teacher	1.4	1.7	.3	1.2	.5	1.4
Service	1.2	1.5	1.7	2.2	2.5	1.7
Technical	4.1	4.5	3.0	1.2	2.2	2.0
Never Worked	.1	.1	.3	.0	.0	.3
Don't Know	6.0	7.5	10.7	13.0	11.6	11.9
Total	1232	1784	299	401	406	294

Mexican-American, while the second and third groups are probably Mexican-American. Catholic schools then one might submit are especially likely to have an effect on relatively more affluent Cuban migrants and on relatively less affluent native-born Mexican-Americans.

TABLE 2.7
Mother's Occupation by Race and Religion
(Percent)

	White		Black		Hispanic	
	Cath.	Non-Cath.	Cath.	Non-Cath.	Cath.	Non-Cath.
Not living with Mother	.7	2.1	1.4	1.3	.8	1.0
Clerical	27.6	24.2	21.4	10.0	17.2	11.5
Craftsman	1.5	1.8	.0	3.1	2.0	2.9
Farmer, Farm Manager	.1	.6	.3	1.5	.3	1.0
Homemaker	13.4	12.3	5.4	12.1	14.4	14.3
Laborer	1.2	2.3	2.0	1.8	2.5	5.2
Manager, Admin.	4.1	4.6	6.1	6.2	3.0	2.8
Military	.2	.1	.0	.3	-	-
Operative	2.6	4.8	3.4	5.9	10.1	9.4
Prof. 1	11.2	6.8	18.3	10.5	6.6	3.5
Proprietor, Owner	1.9	2.6	2.4	.5	3.8	2.4
Protective Service	.3	.3	.7	1.0	-	-
Sales	5.0	5.1	3.1	2.1	5.1	2.4
School Teacher	6.1	6.4	11.2	5.1	6.8	3.5
Service	7.6	9.8	8.5	16.5	8.1	10.5
Technical	1.4	1.1	3.1	1.5	1.5	1.4
Never Worked	7.4	5.5	3.4	3.3	7.1	9.4
Don't Know	7.7	9.8	9.5	17.2	10.9	18.5
Total	1213	1754	295	389	396	286

It is children of the more affluent, better-educated, and more successful minority group members who attend Catholic schools. Their families are smaller, their fathers are less likely to be absent, and if they are Mexican-American they are somewhat more likely to come from immigrant families. We can therefore expect that part of the very large outcome difference in Catholic secondary education is a function of the economics and demography of their background.

TABLE 2.8
Immigration Experience
(Percent)

Respondent	White		Black		Hispanic	
	Public	Catholic	Public	Catholic	Public	Catholic
Born in U.S.	96	95	94	95	83	78
In U.S. for less than 10 years	2	3	4	4	9	9
Father immigrant	11	15	25	19	38	70
Mother immigrant	10	15	18	16	39	68

TABLE 2.9
Academic Performance by Immigration, Father's Education, and Type of School Attended for Hispanic Respondents
(Z Score)

	Public	Catholic
Father immigrant, attended college	-34	+30
Father immigrant, did not attend college.	-38	-24
Father not an immigrant, attended college.	-05	-03
Father not an immigrant, and did not attend college.	-76	-28

EDUCATIONAL ENVIRONMENT IN THE HOME

The affluent American society wants better education for its children since it is precisely through superior education that parents expect to will for their children the advantages they have had in life. Catholic secondary schools have a reputation for being college-preparatory schools, and almost certainly one of the reasons that black or Hispanic parents would choose such schools is that such educational experience would prepare them better for the struggle for college admissions and college degrees. The differences in parental college aspirations between Catholic and public school families are enormous (Table 2.10), and black and Hispanic parents are even more likely to expect their children to graduate from college than are parents of white children who attend Catholic schools (data are available only from the student's estimate of his parents' aspirations in a phase of the High School and Beyond study now being executed—parents are now being interviewed): 77 percent of blacks in Catholic high schools and 70 percent of Hispanics say that their parents expect them to graduate from college (versus slightly more than two-fifths of minority students in public schools), and 35 percent of blacks and 27 percent of Hispanics in Catholic schools say their parents expect them to obtain a Ph.D., M.D., or some similar degree. Catholic schools thus differentiate more sharply than public schools in the college aspirations of black and Hispanic parents than they do in the college aspirations of white parents. Perhaps the principal reason for choosing a Catholic education for one's child if one is a minority family is that the child's chances of graduating from college are perceived as being enhanced by such an educational experience. Black and Hispanic children in Catholic schools are also somewhat more likely to say that their parents supervise their homework and their behavior, though here the differences are not striking. Since most high-school–age young people report high levels of parental supervision of their work, particularly maternal supervision (Table 2.11), the level of homework monitoring seems much higher than one might anticipate. Either there is a lot more parental supervision going on than has been thought, or young people are very generous in their interpretation of the word *monitor*. In subsequent analysis we shall see that it is the college aspiration of the parent and not the monitoring behavior that has an impact on educational outcome.

As one would have anticipated from the more affluent young people who attend Catholic schools, black and Hispanic students in such schools are substantially more likely to have an environment in the home that might be thought to be conducive to learning: a room of their own (not if they are Hispanic, perhaps because of the large size of Hispanic Catholic families), a place to study, an encyclopedia, a daily newspaper, a typewriter, an average library, and a pocket calculator. Blacks in Catholic schools are more likely than whites in Catholic schools to say that they have a place to study, a room of their own, and an encyclopedia. Table 2.12 shows that approximately 9 out of every 10 American secondary students say that there is an encyclopedia in their home and more than two-thirds say that they have a typewriter

TABLE 2.10
Parental College Aspiration for Student by Race and School Type

	Public	Catholic
Percent College Graduate:		
White	44	64
Black	43	77
Hispanic	42	70
Percent with Ph.D.:		
White	11	15
Black	18	35
Hispanic	12	27

(though only 58 percent of public school blacks report they have a typewriter). A very high proportion report having more than 50 books in the family library and owning a pocket calculator. More than 4 out of every 5 young people (excepting blacks and Hispanics in public schools where the proportion is somewhat lower) have one of these transitorized marvels. The minorities who attend Catholic schools then have more physical learning resources around their home than do those who attend public school, but a very substantial proportion of the latter

TABLE 2.11
Parental Supervision
(Percent "True")

	White		Black		Hispanic	
	Public	Catholic	Public	Catholic	Public	Catholic
Father monitors homework	71	78	54	59	64	74
Mother monitors homework	95	89	88	93	85	89
Parents always know what student is doing	79	79	73	78	81	86

TABLE 2.12
Learning Environment
(Percent Have)

	White		Black		Hispanic	
	Public	Catholic	Public	Catholic	Public	Catholic
Place to study	47	55	49	68	45	53
Daily newspaper	82	92	72	82	71	68
Encyclopedia	90	93	85	97	82	91
Typewriter	79	88	58	84	67	85
More than 50 books	86	93	70	93	70	83
Room of your own	82	74	63	77	67	65
Pocket calculator	87	89	67	80	70	83

are also well-endowed with physical resources for learning. Perhaps the most critical factor, especially for blacks, is that less than half of the students (in all three racial/ethnic groups) report that they have a place to study—indeed less say they have a place to study than they have a room of their own, leading one to suspect the "room of your own" does not necessarily mean a room that is exclusively for "your" use, at least in the respondents' interpretation of the meaning of the question.

When the learning environment items are combined into a single factor, large differences between public and Catholic school minority

TABLE 2.13
Learning Environment by Race and School Type
(High = Home Environment Conducive to Learning)

	Public	Catholic
White	00	17
Black	-75	-02
Hispanic	-75	-21

TABLE 2.14
Own College Aspiration in Eighth Grade
(Percent College Graduates)
[Percent Ph.D.s or Similar]

	Public	Catholic
White	43 [9]	64 [24]
Black	46 [12]	77 [24]
Hispanic	38 [8]	66 [17]

students are apparent. Catholic school blacks are three-quarters of a standard deviation higher on the learning environment scale than public school blacks, and Catholic school Hispanics are more than half a standard deviation higher on the same scale than public school Hispanics. Not only are the parents of the Catholic school minority students more likely to expect them to graduate from college, they are also more likely to have created a physical environment in the home conducive to academic achievement.

Catholic school minority students then tend to come from affluent, well-educated families with powerful college aspirations and a physical environment conducive to academic success. Differences on all these measures are so striking that one would be inclined to believe that they measure very critical differences in the family background of public school and Catholic school minority young people.

PERSONAL BACKGROUND

Like their parents, black and Hispanic students in Catholic schools had much higher college and advance degree expectations when they were in eighth grade than their public school counterparts—the differences are approximately 30 percentage points—and minority young people were twice as likely in eighth grade to have already planned for doctorate degrees than minorities who attended public schools (the correlation between parental aspirations and one's own eighth grade aspiration is .60). Young people attending Catholic schools, especially minority young people it would seem, have not been dragged into such

TABLE 2.15
TV Hours by Race and School Type
(Percent 4+ Hours)

	Public	Catholic
White	33	28
Black	49	42
Hispanic	36	30

college-preparatory experience against their will. On the contrary, they appear to be at least as well motivated as their parents to seek higher education and advanced degrees. They are also somewhat less likely to watch more than four hours of TV every week (Table 2.15), though the differences in all three comparison groups are relatively small, indeed much less striking than the differences in homework hours described in the previous chapter. It will turn out in subsequent analysis that once the college aspirations of the student and the parents are taken into account, TV time has little effect on academic achievement.

TABLE 2.16
Students' Use of Time
(Percent Every Day)

	White		Black		Hispanic	
	Public	Catholic	Public	Catholic	Public	Catholic
Visiting with friends	26	27	26	24	24	17
Reading for pleasure	20	21	16	26	17	13
Dating	47	47	43	50	44	52
Driving around	19	15	15	14	16	16
Talking on phone	49	53	54	68	41	56
Thinking	47	53	42	51	43	44
Talking with Parents	17	20	20	23	22	23
Reading news	43	53	37	49	36	35

TABLE 2.17
Time Use by Race and School Type
(High = "Intellectual" Use of Time)

	Public	Catholic
White	-07	13
Black	-16	19
Hispanic	-33	03

There are considerable differences between public school and Catholic school students in the way they use their time (Tables 2.16–2.18). Catholic school students do not avoid typical teenage behavior such as dating, driving around, or talking on the telephone. If anything (Table 2.18), they are higher on the social use of time than their public school counterparts, and they are also higher on the "intellectual" use of time, more likely to read for pleasure, spend time thinking, reading newspapers, and talking with parents. Perhaps they are more apt to do more of everything because they have more resources.

Because of their class background and their greater success in life which such a background seems to guarantee, young people who attend Catholic high schools probably have higher morale than those who attend public high schools and hence are more likely to both do

TABLE 2.18
"Social" Use of Time
(Z Score)

	Public	Catholic
White	09	09
Black	-20	-12
Hispanic	-22	-08

TABLE 2.19
Psychological Well-Being
(Bradburn Scale)

	Public	Catholic
White	-04	03
Black	-05	25
Hispanic	-19	-05

well in school and be satisfied with the school they attended. Using the psychological well-being scale developed by Norman Bradburn, director of the National Opinion Research Center (Table 2.19), we can observe that while there are only marginal differences between Catholic school and public school whites in morale, there are considerable differences between Catholic school blacks and Hispanics and public school blacks and Hispanics with, as one might have expected, the Catholic school young people having higher morale.

It may well be that both the morale and the use of time and even the TV usage measures are in part the result of attending a private high school and not merely an attitude or a characteristic the young person brings to his educational experience from his family environment. Nevertheless, as explained in the previous chapter, we are taking a conservative tilt against the possibility of a school effect. For present purposes, psychological well-being, use of time, and college aspirations of the young person are all assumed personal characteristics he brings from the home to the school and not to be affected in the least by what happens in the school itself.

By way of summary of this chapter, we have found few surprises: families that exercise the option of selecting a private school for their teenagers are more affluent, better educated, more successful, more concerned about education, and their children are much better equipped physically and psychologically for academic success. The question to be answered in subsequent chapters is whether and to what extent these differences explain the differences in homework, academic achievement, and present college aspirations.

3.

Discipline

Previous NORC research[1] has demonstrated that one of the appeals of Catholic schools for the white Catholic parents who use them is that the schools are thought to have much more effective discipline. Similarly, superior discipline in Catholic schools often comes up in conversations with black parents in inner cities as one of the reasons why they choose to send their children to Catholic schools even though they are not Catholic themselves. Roman Catholic religious orders are reputed to be stern disciplinarians, there are much more likely to be elaborate disciplinary codes at Catholic schools—perhaps the authoritarian structure of the Catholic church is better suited to maintaining adolescent discipline. Catholic schools can much more readily expel disciplinary problems than can public schools. One might therefore anticipate at the beginning of an investigation such as this that one of the reasons for the superior academic performance of students who attend Catholic schools is that the latter have much less serious discipline problems than do public schools, particularly public schools in neighborhoods where black and minority children are most likely to live.

Whatever the "discipline factor" is thought to be whether by admiring parents or by educators who explore the importance of the Catholic school impact, such explanations do not themselves tell us why there is superior academic performance. One still has to know what the dynamics are by which discipline leads to better performance. Do young people do better academically in Catholic schools because they are afraid of the awesome disciplinary power of the schools? Do they learn more because they can devote more of their attention in the school environment to academic questions instead of surviving disciplinary hassle (of the sort which was poignantly if altogether too lightly portrayed in the film *My Bodyguard*)? Or are teachers better able to instruct students if their time is less occupied maintaining order among the unruly members of the class?

The difference in disciplinary environments in the two types of schools can be portrayed on the basis of two different reports in the High School and Beyond research project—evaluation of disciplinary environment by principals of the school and by the students themselves. There are very large differences in reports of disciplinary problems by public and Catholic school principals—one of the sharpest differences between public and Catholic schools and not just between ordinary Catholic schools and Catholic minority schools: 70 percent of the public school teachers report absenteeism as a problem and 58 percent report class-cutting as a problem. Only 9 percent of the principals of the regular Catholic schools cite absenteeism and only 2 percent

TABLE 3.1
Problems in Catholic Schools According to Principals
(Percent Serious or Moderate)

	Public	Catholic	Catholic Minority
Student absenteeism	70	9	20
Students cutting class	58	2	2
Physical conflict among students	8	0	0
Physical conflict between students and teachers	7	0	0
Vandalism	33	18	8
Drugs or alcohol	55	28	28
Rape	8	0	5
Weapons	2	0	0
Verbal abuse of teachers	15	2	3

TABLE 3.2
Discipline Problems in School as Reported by Students
(Percent Often Happens)

	White		Black		Hispanic	
	Public	Catholic	Public	Catholic	Public	Catholic
Students talk back to teachers	42	22	39	33	36	17
Don't obey instructions	26	13	30	17	31	11
Fight with each other	24	9	30	9	25	8
Students attach teacher	17	6	28	11	28	6
Truancy	47	8	43	12	49	12

cutting class (20 percent of the principals of minority schools report an absenteeism problem). While there is not much physical conflict among students in public schools (8 percent) or between students and teachers (7 percent), there is none reported in either kind of Catholic school, and there is more vandalism in the ordinary kind of Catholic school (18 percent) than there is in the Catholic minority school (8 percent). Drugs or alcohol are a moderately serious problem in Catholic schools (28 percent), but almost twice as many (55 percent) public school administrators report drugs or alcohol as a problem. Rape, possession of weapons, and verbal abuse of teachers practically never occur according to Catholic school principals.

Similarly students (Table 3.2) in all three kinds of Catholic schools are much less likely to describe situations in which students talk back to teachers, do not obey instructions, fight with each other, attack teachers, cut class, or miss school. There is little difference among any of the kinds of Catholic schools with the single exception of somewhat more backtalk to teachers among blacks in Catholic schools. Catholic schools, as evaluated both by their principals and students, have much less acute disciplinary problems.

On a discipline scale composed of the students' evaluation of disciplinary problems in their school (Table 3.3), approximately a full standard deviation separates the three groups in Catholic schools from their three public school counterparts, a very substantial difference. Catholic schools earn their reputation for much more effective discipline. Furthermore (Table 3.4), while only a minority (less than a fifth) of

TABLE 3.3
Discipline Scale
(High–Low Discipline Problem)

	Public	Catholic
White	−49	43
Black	−50	31
Hispanic	−49	58

American secondary school students have been tardy or absent for more than five days, such behavior is somewhat more likely to occur in public schools than in Catholic schools, whether because of more effective discipline or because of stronger educational motivation.

Young people who attend Catholic schools, especially if they are minority young people, are less likely to have had a disciplinary problem with the school and to have cut class than their public school counterparts. Yet there is no difference in the probability of suspension between public school and Catholic school students. If one might tentatively suggest that a suspension rate is an indicator of what an expulsion rate might be, there is no evidence that drastic disciplinary punishment is required in Catholic schools. It may well be that either those who require drastic action do not show up in Catholic schools at the secondary level or do not last there very long.

Catholic schools have sterner disciplinary regulations. In almost

TABLE 3.4
Students' Absence and Tardiness

| | White | | Black | | Hispanic | |
	Catholic	Public	Catholic	Public	Catholic	Public
Percent more than five days absent	8	18	13	16	12	20
Percent more than five days tardy	10	15	15	17	14	18

TABLE 3.5
Students as Discipline Problem
(Percent "True" This Year)

	White		Black		Hispanic	
	Public	Catholic	Public	Catholic	Public	Catholic
Has had a discipline problem	13	13	23	14	20	17
Has been suspended	10	10	16	17	11	11
Has cut class	37	19	38	15	39	16

nine-tenths of them, the students report both a dress code and smoking rule (Table 3.6), substantially more than do those who attend any of the public schools. However, hall passes are much more likely to be required in public schools and black students in Catholic schools are no more likely than black students in public schools (58 percent versus 57 percent) to say that they are responsible for damage. Catholic schools, therefore, have less disciplinary problems and sterner disciplinary rules, though it remains to be seen whether stern rules have much to do with the absence of a problem.

Eliminating the hall pass dimension from consideration, we see in Table 3.7 the big difference on the regulation index between those who attend Catholic schools and those who attend public schools—which for whites and Hispanics exceeds the standard deviation and for blacks is three-quarters of a standard deviation—approximately the same span

TABLE 3.6
School Regulations

	White		Black		Hispanic	
	Catholic	Public	Catholic	Public	Catholic	Public
Grounds closed at lunch	39	25	44	22	46	22
Students responsible for damage	81	68	58	57	71	55
Hall passes required	58	80	50	89	65	83
Dress code	98	40	85	58	95	45
Smoking rules	91	70	83	63	86	68

TABLE 3.7
Regulation Index*

	Catholic	Public
White	67	−47
Black	32	−46
Hispanic	55	−56

*A factor on which "hall pass" has a low loading.

of difference in regulations as there is a span of difference in disciplinary problems.

Young people themselves in Catholic schools seem relatively satisfied with both the effectiveness and fairness of discipline (anyone who has dealt with teenagers knows how reluctant they are to admit that adults are ever fair). On the question of effectiveness of discipline, there is little difference among the three racial/ethnic groups. More than three-quarters of the young people in Catholic schools say that discipline is either excellent or good, though less than half of those in public schools are willing to express the same vote of confidence in the discipline they encounter. In each of the racial/ethnic categories, at least twice as many Catholic as public school students (three times as many for the white, four times as many for the Hispanics) testify that disciplinary effectiveness is excellent. Approximately half of those in the three Catholic school groups say that the fairness of discipline is either excellent or good as opposed to about two-fifths of those in the public schools. Whether the discipline in Catholic schools is more authoritarian is beyond the scope of the present research. It certainly involves more comprehensive rule making and is much more likely to regulate the dress and smoking behavior of young people. However, its sternness and effectiveness do not make young people in such schools feel that they are the victims of unfairness or injustice. Quite the contrary, they are more likely to rate their schools high on fairness than are those students who attend the less disciplinarily effective public schools.

TABLE 3.8
Evaluation of Effectiveness and Fairness of Discipline by Students
(Percent Excellent—Percent Good + Excellent)

	White Catholic	White Public	Black Catholic	Black Public	Hispanic Catholic	Hispanic Public
Effectiveness	27 (74)	8 (43)	27 (74)	13 (44)	38 (82)	9 (46)
Fairness	16 (50)	6 (40)	11 (48)	9 (40)	18 (58)	8 (44)

When the two evaluations of school discipline are combined into a single scale (Table 3.9), a familiar pattern of differences emerges. Catholic students who are white or black at Catholic schools are two-fifths of a standard deviation more likely to approve the disciplinary system in the school if the latter is Catholic and two-thirds of a standard deviation more likely to approve the discipline if they are Hispanic. Catholic schools receive a very strong vote of confidence in disciplinary policies and procedures from students subjected to such policies and procedures.

Religious orders' reputation for effective discipline is apparently justified (Table 3.10), for on the scale indicating the absence of a disciplinary problem in the school, the religious order schools are rated higher by their students in those Catholic schools which are not owned by a religious order, 20 standardized points for white students, 16 standardized points for black students, and 13 standardized points for Hispanic

TABLE 3.9
Approval of School's Discipline System
(Z Score)

	Public	Catholic
White	-28	23
Black	-20	24
Hispanic	-15	49

TABLE 3.10
Discipline Scores for Religious Order Schools
(Z Score)

	Owned by order	Owned by someone else
White	54	35
Black	42	26
Hispanic	68	55

students. While religious order schools cannot account for all the difference between public and Catholic schools in disciplinary control, they do seem to be even more effective than other Catholic schools at minimizing disciplinary problems.

To what extent can disciplinary differences between public and Catholic schools be accounted for by the backgrounds of the young people who come to such schools? As we have seen in the previous chapter, Catholic students are more likely to come from affluent families and to have more powerful academic motivation. This background and motivation may partly explain why Catholic schools are less likely to have disciplinary problems. Perhaps it is not all that difficult to maintain effective disciplinary control when one has well-trained and motivated students.

The explanatory model in Table 3.11 allows us to investigate possible explanations for the apparently superior disciplinary conditions in Catholic schools. There is for both white and minority students a difference of 94 standardized points (94 percent of a standard deviation) between Catholic and public school attenders in their description of disciplinary conditions at the school. When one takes into account such background variables as an absent father, education and income (combined as "social class"), parental college plans for the student, the students' own college plans, and their use of time, the differences diminish 10 standardized points for minority students and 11 standardized points for white students. Background motivations provide a very limited explanation for differences in disciplinary conditions in Catholic and public schools; and when one adds the extent of rules in the

TABLE 3.11
Model to Explain Differences between Minority Students Attending Catholic and Public Schools in Their Description of the Disciplinary Problem of the School
(Z Score)

	Minority	White
Raw	94	94
Absent father	92	94
Social class	88	89
Parental college plans for student	85	87
Students' college plans	85	86
Students' use of time	85	86
Rules in school	85	85
Student has been a disciplinary problem himself/herself	78	78
Religious order owns school	67	75
Student rating of fairness and effectiveness of discipline	57	74

school, no new explanatory power is added. Catholic schools may have sterner rules, but they do not account for the more effective disciplinary control when social class and motivational factors have already been taken into account.

Public schools are more likely to have disciplinary problems, as the students attending those schools were themselves willing to admit. May not this higher level of disciplinary problem explain much of the remaining difference between the two kinds of schools?

Whether the average student in the school (as represented by our probability sample of students) has been a disciplinary problem in the last year only removes 7 more standardized points from the differences between these two types of institutions. Putting seven possible types of explanations into the model—an absent father, social class, college plans of parents, college plans of students, students' use of time, number of rules in the school, and the typical disciplinary problem—only reduces the differences between the two institutions from a little less than 1 standard deviation to a little bit more than three-quarters of a standard deviation. It would appear that the disciplinary effectiveness of the Catholic school is not merely a matter of a different type of student who enrolls in such schools.

Two more variables were entered into the model: whether a religious order owns the school and student rating of the fairness and effectiveness of discipline. For white students, neither of these variables made an appreciable addition to the explanatory power of the model. For minority students, both made a considerable explanatory contribution. The differences for minorities declined from 78 standardized points to 67 when religious order ownership was taken into account, and to 57 standardized points when the student rating of fairness and effectiveness of discipline was taken into account. Religious order ownership and student attitude toward the disciplinary system then were substantially more important in explaining disciplinary differences between public and Catholic schools for minority young people than for white young people. The explanatory model accounted for about half of the difference in disciplinary atmosphere between Catholic and public schools for minority students, with most of the explanation coming not from the student's background but from religious order ownership of the school and from student rating of the fairness and effectiveness of discipline.

One of the four problems raised in the first chapter is partially solved. As far as minority students are concerned, much of the difference in discipline between public and Catholic schools comes from the effectiveness of the control of a religious order and from the students' own view of the disciplinary system as fair and effective. Some of the explanation can be attributed to the students' background and motivations, but a substantial component of the explanation must be contributed by factors internal to the school and its disciplinary system. The model offers only a partial explanation; more than half a standard deviation difference remains between public and Catholic schools unaccounted for by our explanation, even after our nine-variable model has been applied. The effectiveness of Catholic schools' disciplinary system merits more detailed study. It is not sufficient to say that Catholic schools can expel their disciplinary problems. At least as high a proportion of those still in Catholic schools had disciplinary problems in the previous year as did those in public schools. What may be the case is that Catholic schools are able to expel their extreme disciplinary problems. It does not take many young people to create a difficult and even dangerous disciplinary climate in a school. Fighting with each other, attacking teachers, talking back to teachers, refusing to obey instructions—can utterly disrupt the morale and effectiveness of an institution, even when done by only a handful of young people. It may be that Catholic schools simply do not permit such a handful of young people to disrupt their school and can eliminate them from their student body without necessarily having a very high expulsion rate, for if only one out of every seven or eight young people have any kind of disciplinary problem, perhaps only one in twenty-five or even one in fifty might create a serious disciplinary problem (but one in fifty can easily disrupt an institution). In a school of a thousand students, the expulsion of one in fifty would only lead to the dismissal from that institution of twenty students in the course of a year, hardly enough for anyone to notice, though their absence might have an enormous positive impact on the student body. There is no information from Catholic schools to test this hypothesis, which ought to be investigated more fully. If one cannot account for the remaining disciplinary differences between the two types of institutions by a somewhat higher (though still rather small) expulsion rate, then one would certainly want to take a closer look at the disciplinary methods and style of Catholic secondary schools to see what it is that makes them so effective.

We are assuming that discipline makes for effective teaching and not vice versa, since my conservative perspective is aimed at minimizing instructional differences between Catholic and public schools and seeking an explanation outside of the classroom experience until forced to take a look at what goes on inside the classroom. In the real world, there is a reciprocal flow of influence between teaching effectiveness and discipline. If the teacher is perceived as confident and interested and thus able to maintain the students' attention, the students will be somewhat less likely to be a disciplinary problem. On the other hand, the less likely that a teacher will have disciplinary problems, the easier it is for him or her to be an effective and interested teacher. If the remarkable disciplinary and academic success of Catholic secondary educational institutions leads researchers to examine them far more carefully than they have in the past, the complex issue of the relationship between teaching and discipline would have to be explored in more intricate detail than is possible in the present enterprise.

Disciplinary problems then are much less likely to occur in Catholic schools. Such institutions have more rules and regulations, but the regulations do not account for the differences in disciplinarian atmosphere. Young people in Catholic schools give far higher ratings to the fairness and effectiveness of the disciplinary system, and for minority young people this is an important part of the difference in disciplinary atmosphere. Ownership of a school by a religious order also makes a contribution to the difference in the description of the disciplinary environment by minority students. Family background and the personal motivation of the student make some contribution toward explaining differences between the disciplinary environment in Catholic and public schools, but as far as minority students are concerned, family and personal background variables are less important than religious order ownership and young people's evaluation of the fairness and the effectiveness of discipline.

NOTE

1. Andrew Greeley and Peter Rossi, "Education and Catholic Americans"; Andrew Greeley, William McCready, and Kathleen McCourt, "Catholic Schools and the Declining Church."

4.

Academics

We saw in the first chapter the considerable differences between those who attend Catholic schools and public schools in academic performance, amount of time spent on homework, and college aspirations. In chapter 2 we noted the substantial differences in background and motivation which distinguish students in the two kinds of schools, and that in addition the students report rather different disciplinary environments. In this chapter we will examine in greater detail the different academic environment and outcome of Catholic and public secondary schools.

The academic performance index which is a combination of reading and two mathematics test scores also reflects differences in vocabulary, science, civics, and writing skills that exist in Catholic and public schools—regardless of racial and ethnic origin. Approximately a quarter of a standard deviation separates whites in Catholic schools from whites in public schools, and approximately half a standard deviation separates the minority group young people in the two schools. We will defer until chapter 6 a detailed explanation of these differences.

Young people in Catholic schools, whatever their racial or ethnic background, seem to like their schools or at least to give them a high rating not only on the fairness and effectiveness of discipline, but also and especially on the quality of instruction and teacher interest. Black and white youths are as likely to rate public and Catholic schools as

TABLE 4.1
Achievement Test Scores by Race and Type of School Attended
(Z Score)

	Vocabulary Catholic Public		Reading Catholic Public		Math 1 Catholic Public		Math 2 Catholic Public	
White	32	-05	21	00	25	00	15	-03
Black	-39	-93	-27	-77	-46	-87	-36	-63
Hispanic	-12	-75	-18	-73	-23	-71	-16	-47

	Science Catholic Public		Writing Catholic Public		Civics Catholic Public		Academic Performance* Catholic Public	
White	21	12	31	00	23	-04	25	-01
Black	-58	-96	-37	-91	-13	-66	-44	-91
Hispanic	-29	-69	-16	-65	-11	-52	-23	-77

*Reading + Math 1 + Math 2.

excellent in building and library facilities, though Hispanic students give higher marks to Catholic schools even in these matters. There is surprisingly little difference between the descriptions of teaching and discipline in Catholic schools and in public schools across all three racial/ethnic groups. Catholic school students are at least twice as likely to rate the quality of instruction, teacher interest, and the effec-

TABLE 4.2
Rating of the School
(Percent Excellent)

	White Public Catholic		Black Public Catholic		Hispanic Public Catholic	
Building	16	17	16	14	13	22
Library	20	16	21	19	19	18
Quality of instruction	11	28	13	24	10	31
Teacher interest	10	25	11	23	12	28
Effectiveness of discipline	8	27	10	28	6	34
Fairness of discipline*	37	49	34	46	39	55

*Excellent + good.

TABLE 4.3
Quality of Instruction
(Z Score)

	Public	Catholic
White	-.33	.28
Black	-.47	.15
Hispanic	-.38	.34

*Students rating of interest and ability of teachers.

tiveness and fairness of discipline as "excellent." They are much more satisfied with their experience in the schools they attend and hence alert us to the possibility that the differential experience and background of public school students must be taken into account in explaining the difference in educational outcomes.

When the student's reaction to the quality of instruction and teacher interest is combined into a scale which we will call the "quality of instruction" scale (Table 4.3), it develops that more than three-fifths of a standard deviation separates the rating of their institutions by those in Catholic schools from the rating of those in public schools. In ordinary sociological research, differences of this dimension are thought to be very striking indeed—the experienced researcher is usually inclined to check his data when he discovers such a difference. One more often thinks that differences of such a magnitude are the result of computational error, or perhaps the confusion of a correlation with a definition. There were no computational errors in the production of Table 4.4, and no one has seriously suggested that by definition the quality of instruction in Catholic schools will be better than that in public schools.

There are a number of other measures of academic experience of the secondary student (Tables 4.4 and 4.5), in which Catholic schools also receive higher ratings, especially from minority young people. Those who attend Catholic schools are more likely to say that they have participated in laboratory work or in field projects, that they have written

TABLE 4.4
Participation in Laboratory Work or Other Projects
(Percent Frequently or Fairly Often)

	Catholic	Public
White	44	42
Black	53	40
Hispanic	45	37

essays, poems, or term papers for their classes, that they have received individual instruction, and that they are satisfied with the academic effort made by their high school. As we shall see in chapter 7, Catholic schools have less teachers per student with lower academic credentials, and pay them less than public school teachers. However, they apparently are better able to provide for their students the opportunities, challenges, support, and resources necessary for a successful secondary educational experience.

Catholic school teachers also either demand or obtain more homework (Table 4.8). In all three racial and ethnic groups students in Catholic schools are twice as likely to report that they do more than five hours of homework a week than their public school counterparts. Homework, like many other indicators of academic environment we are using in this study, differs much more dramatically between Catholic and public schools than among blacks, whites, and Hispanics. Catholic schools apparently are able to impose the same kinds of academic and disciplinary demands, and provide the same kinds of academic and disciplinary resources for members of all three racial and ethnic groups. The difference between whites and, for example, blacks, in Catholic schools are either nonexistent, as in the case of homework, writing papers, or satisfaction with teacher interest and instructional quality, or substantially less than in public schools. Thus, while whites in Catholic schools may receive higher scores than blacks in Catholic schools, the margin that separates the two is not as large as in public schools.

TABLE 4.5
Writing of Papers, Essays, Poems
(Percent Frequently or Fairly Often)

	Catholic	Public
White	73	60
Black	78	64
Hispanic	79	57

TABLE 4.6
Individual Instruction
(Percent Frequently or Fairly Often)

	Catholic	Public
White	25	25
Black	41	35
Hispanic	36	30

TABLE 4.7
Satisfaction with High School Academic Effort
(Percent Very Satisfied)

	Catholic	Public
White	39	25
Black	29	17
Hispanic	36	18

TABLE 4.8
Hours of Homework per Week
(Percent More Than Five Hours per Week)

	Catholic	Public
White	42	23
Black	44	22
Hispanic	44	22

Catholic school students from each of the three ethnic groups are more likely to have an A or B grade point average; 7 percentage points more likely if they are white or black and 9 percentage points more likely if they are Hispanic (Table 4.9). And, as we have seen in chapter 2, they are substantially more likely to expect that they will graduate from college, an expectation which the apparently superior quality of their instruction and their better academic performance seems to justify.

Catholic school graduates regardless of ethnic background are twice as likely to plan preprofessional curriculum in their college plans (Table 4.11). They are also somewhat more likely to plan a business major, which may indicate—especially in the current conditions of the marketplace—expectations of upward mobility.

The greater academic demand, superior academic achievement, and more powerful academic and occupational intentions of students in Catholic schools do not seem to interfere with their participation in

TABLE 4.9
Grade Point Average
(Percent "A's" or "A's" and "B's")

	White	Black	Hispanic
Public	32	16	21
Catholic	39	23	30

TABLE 4.10
College Graduation Expectations
(Percent Expect to Graduate from College)

	Public	Catholic
White	43	64
Black	48	77
Hispanic	38	66

extracurricular activities (Table 4.12). Blacks are more likely to be active in such activities than whites (especially in sports activities), and Hispanics less likely than whites, but in each of the three ethnic categories there is little difference between those who attend public schools and those who attend Catholic schools. The superiority of academic environment and academic outcome in Catholic institutions has not produced situations in which all work and no play have made Jack a dull boy and Jill a dull girl (or Juan or Juanita, for that matter). The

TABLE 4.11
College Major

	Public	Catholic
White		
Business	17.9	21.0
Preprofessional	5.4	10.0
Black		
Business	15.3	19.9
Preprofessional	6.3	11.4
Hispanic		
Business	18.9	22.5
Preprofessional	4.6	9.0

TABLE 4.12
Student Activities
(Percent Participate)

	White		Black		Hispanic	
	Public	Catholic	Public	Catholic	Public	Catholic
Varsity sports	33	35	38	45	29	30
Other sports	45	54	48	56	43	42
Cheer leaders, etc.	15	15	20	21	12	17
Subject matter clubs	24	27	31	30	28	30
Vocational ed. clubs	4	1	22	5	22	5
Community youth clubs	21	26	27	31	12	22
Church groups	40	35	47	46	25	32
Junior achievement	4	6	16	16	8	8
Band	17	6	16	12	10	9
Chorus or dance	20	20	30	40	19	25
Hobby clubs	21	22	25	26	17	23
Honor societies	18	24	15	16	14	18
Newspaper	18	30	21	27	17	23
Student government	16	18	25	29	15	20
Activity scale (Z score)	−03	−08	26	25	−21	−14

apparent academic success of Catholic schools has not been achieved at the cost of or diminished the importance of other aspects of human life.

We will defer until chapter 6 our discussion of the three remaining "problems" of Catholic education—homework, college aspirations, and academic performance. But before this discussion of the academic environment of secondary schools is complete, two questions remain: (1) To what extent can the difference in grade point average between Catholic and public school students be accounted for by greater effort on the part of Catholic school students? (2) Can we explain in terms of different familial and personal backgrounds of students attending the different kinds of schools the difference in their reaction to the instruction received?

Minority students in Catholic schools are some 15 percentage points more likely to say that their grade point averages are in the A or mostly A and B range. Approximately half of that difference can be accounted

TABLE 4.13
Model to Explain Different Graduate Point Average between Minority
Students Who Go to Catholic Schools and Public Schools
(Proportion with at Least "B" Average)

Raw difference	15
Homework	07
API	03[*]

[*]Difference no longer significant

for by the fact that Catholic school students do more homework (Table 4.13). The difference descends into statistical insignificance when one takes into account the higher academic performance index of those who attend Catholic schools. Minority students in Catholic secondary educational institutions deserve the better grades they receive compared to their counterparts in public schools. The difference in grade point averages can be accounted for by the fact that the Catholic school minority young people do more homework and have learned more (insofar as scores on standardized achievement tests can be considered a measure of learning).

A more complex and fascinating question is whether the difference between the perceived quality of instruction (including both teacher competence and teacher interest) in Catholic and public schools might be a function not of what actually has happened in the schools but of the background characteristics a student brings. It is not unreasonable to expect that young people coming from more affluent family backgrounds are more strongly influenced both by their own and their parents' college plans and will be more likely to find the teaching they receive to be "excellent." For if you are strongly motivated to learn from teachers you are more likely to listen to them and be impressed by what they know. For such young people the teacher has information and skills necessary to further their plans. The student who is more strongly motivated should strike an implicit bargain with the teacher in which the student gives higher levels of attention in return for which the teacher provides better instruction.

TABLE 4.14
Model to Explain Differences between Students Attending Catholic and Public
Schools in Their Rating of the Quality of Instruction
(Z Score)

	Minority	White
Raw difference	71	64
Social class	65	56
Parental college plans for student	60	52
Students' college aspiration in 8th grade	57	40
Owned by religious order	46	38
Discipline problems in school	25	.13

Such background factors explain part of the difference between the perception of academic environment (and presumably the actual academic environment) in public and Catholic schools—whether by white or minority young people. Parental education, occupation, income, college aspirations, and students' own college aspirations account for 14 of the 71 standardized points which separate minority teenagers in Catholic schools from those in public schools. Another 9 points can be accounted for merely by the fact that the school is owned by a religious order, something which is hardly an aspect of the family or personal background of the student, and another 19 points of the difference can be accounted for by different disciplinary environments in Catholic and public schools (the pattern is similar for white students, though disciplinary environment seems to make more difference for them than for black students).

A substantial difference remains even after disciplinary factors are taken into account between the academic environment of public and Catholic schools for minority young people. A superior academic environment—as perceived by the student—is not merely a function of the more benign disciplinary situation. Nor can one account for the different evaluations of academic quality of Catholic schools in terms of student background. Religious order ownership and the disciplinary environment are far more important than the characteristics and attributes students bring to the school. Something seems to be going on in Catholic schools independently of home background which accounts for the superior evaluation of the quality of instruction in such schools. Young peoples' perception of the quality cannot be written off as merely subjective. While one is dealing here with probabilities as in all social research, one must also say that the probabilities are quite high. On the average the quality of instruction in Catholic schools is better than in public schools for blacks and Hispanics, but also for white students.

The pieces of the puzzle are now in place. Students who go to Catholic high schools come from more affluent and educationally ambitious family backgrounds and have more powerful personal motivations. But they also go to schools where both the disciplinary and academic environments seem to be objectively superior. The academic outcomes—academic performance, homework, grade point average (which is a function of homework and academic performance), and college aspirations—are all higher in Catholic schools. The question posed in the first chapter can now be posed more precisely: To what extent is the more impressive outcome the result of this familial and personal input and to what extent is it the result of different disciplinary and academic environments in the schools themselves? In chapter 6 we will attempt to answer these questions after pausing in chapter 5 to consider the religious environment of the Catholic school and the possibility that this too may influence the academic outcome of Catholic secondary education.

5.

Religion and the Catholic School

Catholic schools were not initially designed to be educationally superior. They came into existence for specifically religious purposes—to protect or enhance religious faith and practice of young Catholics while facilitating their educational and occupational mobility in American society. While occasionally the more militant supporters of Catholic schools may have argued that they were educationally better, the normal stance in the Catholic community has been that Catholic schools are "as good" educationally as public schools. At one time many "liberal" self-critics in American Catholicism felt that Catholic schools were probably educationally inferior to public schools. If it now develops that Catholic schools are academically superior, this may cause some rejoicing in Catholic circles but it does not answer the question of whether Catholic secondary schools have a religious impact of the sort for which they were designed.

The present project was not organized to evaluate the religious outcome of Catholic education. Three other NORC reports in the last two decades ("The Education of Catholic Americans," "Catholic Schools and the Declining Church," and "The Young Catholic Adult") have considered this question and have reported that Catholic education, particularly Catholic secondary education, seems to make a moderate contribution to higher levels of Catholic activity and devotion, even when family background is taken into account. The more pertinent

53

TABLE 5.1
Religion

	White		Black		Hispanic	
	Public	Catholic	Public	Catholic	Public	Catholic
Percent Catholic	30	92	4	50	73	96
Percent "very religious"	10	14	6	12	13	15
Percent church services every week	43	71	50	44	45	53
Percent of Catholics who attend every week	53	67	45	45	43	52
"Some" birth control information	75	75	68	82	75	71
Birth control information from school	26	29	27	33	30	30
"Lot" of birth control information (women)	23	22	35	40	21	23
Percent politically "conservative"	7	7	9	8	10	11
Percent politically "liberal" or "radical"	20	20	20	25	21	10

question for the present research is whether devotion or church affiliation have any effect on academic achievement. Might it be that in an upwardly mobile Catholic community, the more devout are the more ambitious, or the more ambitious are the more devout?

The majority of young people in Catholic schools are Catholic (Table 5.1), though half of the blacks in Catholic schools are not. White Catholics who attend parochial schools are substantially more likely to attend church services than white Catholics in public schools, but the differences are much more modest among Hispanics and simply do not exist among blacks. Those who attend Catholic schools are more likely to possess birth control information and even more likely to say that the information has come from the school. It does not seem likely that the difference between minorities in Catholic schools and those in public schools can be accounted for either by superior religious devotion or superior Catholic morality (and what little regard there seems to be for the church's birth control teaching in Catholic secondary schools).

Nor is there any evidence of greater political conservatism in Catholic schools. Within each of the three groups there is little difference in the proportion describing themselves as conservative in both Catholic

TABLE 5.2
Attitudes on Role of Women
(Percent)

| | White | | | | Black | | | | Hispanic | | | |
| | Men | | Women | | Men | | Women | | Men | | Women | |
	Pub-lic	Cath-olic	Pub-lic	Cath-olic	Pub-lic	Cath-olic	Pub-lic	Cath-olic	Pub-lic	Cath-olic	Pub-lic	Cath-olic
Working mother (approve)	60	51	66	59	80	68	75	90	68	64	75	74
Woman as housekeeper (disapprove)	36	41	62	67	42	51	52	88	38	41	44	53
Woman happiest in home (disagree)	44	50	64	64	39	49	44	57	47	42	47	53

and public schools. Catholic school blacks are more likely to describe themselves as politically liberal or radical; Catholic school Hispanics somewhat less likely to do so.

Those who attend Catholic schools (Table 5.2) are more likely to approve feminism or reject antifeminist stands (especially if they are blacks) than are those who attend public schools. When the three feminist items are combined into a single scale (Table 5.3), there is little difference between public and Catholic school whites, Catholic school blacks are much more likely to be feminist, and Hispanic women in Catholic schools are more likely to be feminist than Hispanic women in public schools, while the exact reverse is true for Hispanic men.

There are signs then of greater religious devotion, particularly among whites who attend Catholic schools, but no signs of greater acceptance of the church's birth control teachings. Nor is there any evidence that Catholic school young people are more conservative than those who attend public school, either in matters of political self-

TABLE 5.3
"Feminist" Scale by Sex
(Z Score—High = Pro Feminist)

| | Men | | Women | |
	Public	Catholic	Public	Catholic
White	-33	-26	28	25
Black	-33	-05	05	72
Hispanic	-18	-28	03	13

description or in feminist attitude. Blacks in Catholic schools are more likely to be both more liberal politically and profeminist (perhaps because of family background and not because of the schools attended).

None of these matters—religious devotion, importance of religion, Catholic church affiliation, attitudes on birth control, feminism, and politics—correlate with academic performance. The present brief chapter is useful for disposing of some possible myths about the conservatism which might be expected to be the result of the sterner Catholic disciplinary environment. It does not add any new pieces to the puzzle of more impressive academic outcomes in Catholic schools because there is no statistically significant correlation between any of these variables and academic performance.

6.

Solutions

With all the pieces of the puzzle apparently in place, we must now determine whether we really have a solution. Three key phenomena must be kept in mind:

1. The academic outcomes of Catholic secondary education for minority groups are impressively superior to those of public education for the same groups. Those attending Catholic high school are 20 percentage points more likely to do homework that requires at least 5 hours a week, 29 percentage points more likely to be confident of college graduation, and to score more than half a standard deviation higher on a standardized academic achievement scale.

2. Young people who attend Catholic schools come from very different family backgrounds than those who attend public schools, and also have very different personal characteristics. Their families are more affluent, better educated, more determined that the young people should have college educations, and more likely to surround the student with the physical appurtenances that facilitate success. The student is more likely to have planned college since eighth grade, and to make more effective intellectual use of the time available to him or her.

3. There are some aspects of the Catholic educational environment that cannot be accounted for merely in terms of student background characteristics. At this point, the disciplinary and academic environment of Catholic schools seems objectively superior, not merely the result of recruiting a

different kind of student. Ownership of some Catholic schools by religious communities—which can hardly be thought to be the result of parental or student choice—seems to have a strong effect on academic and disciplinary environments.

The most important question about these three propositions is whether the first can be explained entirely or almost entirely by the second, or whether the third proposition also must be adduced to provide an explanation for the first. Do the academic and disciplinary environments of Catholic schools make a contribution to their academic outcomes above and beyond that which can be accounted for by the different background characteristics of their students? And if indeed there is a school contribution to academic outcome above and beyond the input characteristics of family and students—is this result primarily a contribution of superior disciplinary environment, and perhaps also superior community effectiveness produced by religious orders? Or does quality of instruction—the competence and interest of the teacher as evaluated by the students—make a contribution of its own even beyond that of the superior disciplinary environments of Catholic schools?

Briefly we shall find that the difference in college aspiration can be explained almost entirely by background characteristics, but the differences in the academic performance index and amount of homework apparently require us to tilt in the direction of a real school effect—and indeed an instructional effect that goes beyond the disciplinary effectiveness of Catholic schools and even beyond the special influence of religious order ownership.

We begin the final phase of the solution to the problem of Catholic secondary schools with a consideration of the simple correlations between the variable in the model presented in chapter 1 and the three measures of academic outcome. In Table 6.1 certain variables have been dropped from the model—father-absent family, number of siblings, number of hours devoted to television, psychological well-being, and parental monitoring of homework. All these variables correlated with academic outcome at a level lower than .15 and had made no contribution to explaining differences between Catholic and public schools once prior variables have been taken into account in the model. They were therefore discarded from the final analysis.

The remaining ten components of the model all correlate strongly

TABLE 6.1
Simple Correlations (r) between Variables in Explanatory Model and
Educational Outcomes

	Academic Performance	Home-work	Current College Plans
Income	.31	.15	.23
Father's education	.31	.19	.32
Mother's education	.26	.21	.33
Parental college expectation for student	.35	.25	.60
Learning environment	.30	.18	.26
Student's 8th grade college plans	.25	.23	.46
Use of time	.29	.24	.28
Religious order ownership	.20	.23	.46
Quality of instruction	.33	.28	.28
Disciplinary environment	.23	.22	.23

with academic performance, hours of homework, and current college plans. Half of the ten variables correlate at a level higher than .3 and all the others higher than .2 with academic performance. Seven of the correlations with homework were in excess of .12 and the other two in excess of .15. The relative magnitude of the respective correlations in the first two rows is similar—in both cases, for example, quality of instruction is the strongest correlate of the outcome. The third row is strikingly different. The two largest correlates of a young person's current college plans are parental college expectations (.60) and his/her own plans in eighth grade, recalled retrospectively (.46).

First we will attempt to explain the fact that minority young people attending Catholic secondary schools are 21 percentage points more likely to spend more than five hours on homework each week (Table 6.2). For the purposes of this analysis, homework has been put in 0-1 categories with a score of 1 attributed to a respondent who has done more than five hours of homework during the week and a score of 0 is

TABLE 6.2
**Model to Explain Differences between Those Who Attend Catholic and Public
School in Their Propensity to Do More Than Five Hours of Homework a Week
(Percent)**

	Minor	White
Raw difference	21	19
Social class	20	15
College aspiration of parent	18	13
Learning environment	17	13
College aspiration in 8th grade	16	12
Use of time	14	11
Administered by religious order	10	10
Quality of instruction*	03	07

*Difference no longer significant

TABLE 6.3
**Model to Explain Differences between Public and Catholic Secondary School
Students in Confidence of College Graduation
(Percent)**

	White	Minority
Raw difference	24	29
Income	21	27
Parental education	19	23
Parental college plans for student	09	10
Learning environment	80	10
Student's 8th grade plans	05	08
Use of time	04	06
Quality of instruction*	02	03

*Not significant

less than five hours. Thus the B in a regression equation represents percentage points difference between Catholic and public school students.

The 21 percentage points difference between Catholic school minority students and public school minority students is diminished to 20 percentage points when the income and education of parents is taken into account, to 18 percentage points when the college aspiration of parents is considered, to 17 percentage points when the home learning environment is added to the model, and to 16 percentage points when the college expectation of the student in eighth grade is taken into account. Finally, 14 percentage points difference remains when we add to the model our knowledge of how the young person uses his/her time. In other words, one-third of the difference between minority young people in Catholic schools and those in public schools in their propensity to do homework can be accounted for by family and personal background variables. But two-thirds of the difference remains unexplained. If one then builds into the model two forces which are

TABLE 6.4
Table Models to Explain Differences between Public and Catholic School Students in Academic Achievement
(Z Score)

	Blacks	Hispanics	Whites	Minority Poor**
Raw difference	50	54	26	53
Family				
Income	41	45	19	47
Parental education	37	38	15	40
College aspiration	27	30	13	33
Learning environment	26	27	12	31
Student				
College aspiration in 8th grade	25	26	10	30
Use of time	21	22	09	21
School				
Quality of instruction	04*	.05*	02*	.07*

*Difference no longer statistically significant

**Minority poor are whites and blacks in the lowest third of income for these groups--under $12,000

surely to be considered part of the school environment—ownership by a religious order and the quality of academic instruction—the difference descends from 14 percentage points to 3 and becomes statistically insignificant. The remaining two-thirds of the difference seems to be the result of dynamics that tilt us in the direction of a school outcome explanation for the homework differential.

The model is parallel to but somewhat different from the one that seems to operate for white young people. Religious order ownership and quality of instruction add not 11 percentage points to the explanation as they do for minority students but only 4 percentage points to the explanation, and the residual difference of 7 percentage points in homework done by whites in Catholic schools in comparison to whites in public schools remains statistically significant. The important point

TABLE 6.5
Relationship between Religious Order Ownership, Discipline, and Quality of Instruction with Academic Performance Index for Minority Students (All Schools)

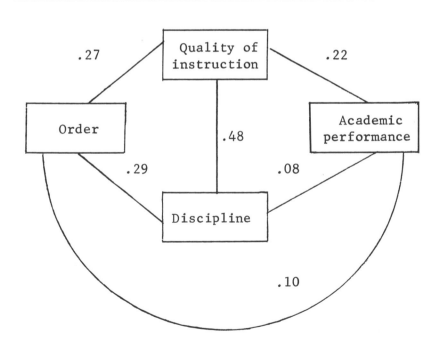

TABLE 6.6
**Attendance at High Schools with More Than 500 Students by School Type for
Whites and Minorities
(Percent in High School over 500)**

	White	Minority
Catholic	72	61
Public	88	91

(Table 6.6) is that the homework differential among minority young people in Catholic schools seems not to be an input effect but a school environment effect.

The opposite set of dynamics seem to be at work when we attempt to account for the difference in confidence of college graduation between Catholic and public school students. For blacks and Hispanics the simple difference between those in Catholic schools and those in public schools in confidence they will graduate from college is 29 percentage points. Family income reduces the difference to 27 percentage points, and parental education to 23. When parental college plans for student is added, the difference drops dramatically to 10 percentage points, and learning environment in the home as well as students' own college aspirations when they were in eighth grade reduces the difference still more to 6 percentage points. In other words, 23 of the 29 percentage points difference between Catholic school blacks and Hispanics and public school blacks and Hispanics can be accounted for by the background characteristics of the student. When quality of instruction is added it explains only 3 percentage points more of the difference and reduces the remaining difference to statistical insignificance (a roughly parallel explanation seems to work for white young people too). It would appear that there are two kinds of differences between Catholic and public school minority students. One sort of difference, represented by college aspirations, is an input phenomenon and the school makes only a marginal contribution to accounting for the differences between Catholic school and public school students.

Another set of differences—such as homework time—which occur in Catholic schools can be partly attributed to background characteristics of the student but in greater part seem to be the result of an authentic school effect—or at least incline us to tilt in that direction. The payoff issue is academic performance. Is the very substantial difference on the standardized achievement test (developed by the Educational Testing Service) between Catholic school and public school students primarily a function of family background, or is there an apparently decisive contribution also made by the school environment? The answer seems to be (Table 6.4) that a little more than half the difference can be attributed to family background but a little less than half seems to be attributable to school environment effect and can be explained almost totally by considering the quality of academic instruction.

Parental social class factors reduce the difference from 50 standardized points to 37 for blacks and from 54 to 38 for Hispanics. The college aspirations of parents and the learning environment in the home cut the differences again to 26 standardized points for blacks and 27 for Hispanics. If one takes into account the eighth grade college aspirations of the young person and his/her use of time, the remaining difference for blacks is 21 standardized points and for Hispanics 22. Input characteristics, then, from the family, from the personal motivation habits of the young person notably diminish the difference between public school minority students and Catholic school minority students in their academic performance (and for white students they diminish the differences from 26 standardized points to 9). In all groups the addition to the model of the quality of academic instruction variable reduces the difference to statistical insignificance. Even after one has taken into account the social class and motivational background of the student, there is still a substantial amount of the difference in academic performance between Catholic school and public school students that can be accounted for by the superior academic environment of Catholic secondary schools. The difference is especially striking for the "poor" in the minority groups (those whose family income is less than $12,000 and hence are in the lower one-third of families in the High School and Beyond sample). Half of the difference of 53 points in the academic performance of the minority poor in Catholic and public schools can be attributed to background variables, but the other half of the difference is associated with the quality of academic instruction which reduces the difference between the two groups once more to statistical insignificance.

Almost the same results can be obtained if one removes academic environment from the model and replaces it with disciplinary environment. One can account for the differences between Catholic and public school students over and above the difference which can be attributed to family background by invoking either the superior disciplinary environment of the Catholic school or its superior instructional environment.

Which of the two Catholic school dynamics is more important—quality of instruction or discipline—especially since they are related to one another? It would be possible to investigate this question by putting both variables in together (and adding the religious order variable) in Table 6.4. Such a strategy would require a changing of sign and introduce greater complexity than perhaps is appropriate for this report. A subsequent table will enable us to accomplish the same purpose without having to change the sign from plus to minus at the foot of the table. One can readily sort out the functioning of the three Catholic school environmental forces by using the standardized correlation coefficients (betas) as in Table 6.5. About half of the influence of the religious order on academic performance is filtered through the fact that religious order schools have both higher quality instruction and more effective discipline—and each of the intervening variables, discipline and instruction, seem equally important in their channeling function for the impact of the religious order. The other half of the religious order effect operates independently of quality of instruction and discipline and has a direct effect on academic performance, a direct effect marginally larger than that of disciplinary environment (a beta of .10 versus a beta of .08). Table 6 shows that the quality of academic instruction is more important than both disciplinary control and religious order ownership when the effects of all three are taken into account together. Disciplinary control in Catholic schools is important but it is not as important as the quality of academic instruction (as perceived by the student) and much less is the quality of instruction merely a surrogate for an effect that is essentially disciplinary. There is no support in Table 6.5 for the argument that the reason for the higher academic performance of those who go to Catholic schools is not better classroom instructional experience but more effective disciplinary control. Quite the contrary, classroom instruction seems to be more important than disciplinary control when the two are considered simultaneously.

Our solution to the Catholic school problem strongly tilts us toward a school effect explanation, at least for the difference in homework and academic performance, if not for the difference in college aspirations. As Coleman and his colleagues point out in their study of private schools, one can never exclude the possibility that some parental or familial effect which we have not considered and statistically standardized may still be at work and may be masked by the apparent impact of school discipline, instructional quality, and religious order ownership. We therefore began to search for a school characteristic which might vary the strength of the findings and at the same time might be considered a most unlikely dimension of parental choice. One candidate for such a characteristic was school size. Presumably minority parents would choose a Catholic high school that was nearby or perhaps one that had an impressive academic reputation. It did not seem very probable that parents would take the size of the school into serious consideration. We were inclined to think before the fact that the Catholic schools would tend to be among the smaller ones (because of research done by Donald Light at NORC in the middle 1960s in which some effects of Catholic education—most notably on integration of disadvantaged students into the school community—seem to be concentrated especially among the small schools). Minority students in Catholic schools (Table 6.6) were much less likely to be attending a school with more than 500 students than were minority students in public schools (61 percent versus 91 percent), so there is a structural difference in size between Catholic schools and public schools which racial/ethnic minorities attend (and also a difference, although not as large, for white students). But the finding went in the opposite direction than that we had anticipated. The difference between Catholic and public school minority young people in academic performance is especially strong among those who attend large schools (Table 6.7). In schools with less than 500 students, minority members who attend public schools are 84 standardized points beneath the mean of the population being analyzed, while those who attend Catholic schools are 47 points beneath the mean, a difference of 36 standardized points. In large schools, the difference was 81 standardized points and 18 standardized points—or 63 standardized points separating the academic achievement scores of Catholic school and public school students. Another way of describing the phenomenon shown in Table 6.7 is that students who attend large schools routinely score higher on the academic performance index than students who attend small schools, unless they happen to be minority students in public schools. In such cases the

TABLE 6.7
Academic Performance by School Size, School Type, and Race
(Z Scores)

School Type	White		Minority	
	Small School	Large School	Small School	Large School
Catholic	02	19	-47	-18
Public	-28	-08	-84	-81

large school does not seem to have its characteristic effect of improving the academic achievement score.

This reversal of our expectations seems to strengthen the case for the notion that the structural dimension which is constituted by its size is not likely to be an object of parental choice. Parents might well choose a smaller school on the argument that the youth will receive more attention in the small school; it is unlikely that minority parents will choose a large school because of the conviction that academic performance is better in large schools (since it is not better in large public schools for such families).

When one varies a structural dimension of the school that is not very likely to be the object of parental choice one varies the impact of the Catholic school effect, suggesting somewhat more strongly that the effect is partly a school effect and not merely the result of parental choice. Furthermore (Table 6.8), the background variables eliminate about as many standardized points in the differences for the students in large schools as they do for students in all schools. The raw difference is diminished 25 points from 63 to 38 when parental income, education, college aspirations, family learning environment, the college plans of the student when he/she was in eighth grade, and use of time are taken into account. But the remaining 38 points diminish to statistical insignificance when the three Catholic school environmental factors are entered into the model—28 points when religious order is taken into account, 22 points when the quality of discipline is taken into account, and to 13 points (and insignificance) when the quality of instruction is taken into account. If one puts instruction in before discipline, instruction diminishes the remaining difference some 12 points and discipline only 7 additional points. Instruction seems to be about

TABLE 6.8
Model to Explain Difference between Public School and Catholic School
Minority Young People in Academic Performance for Those Who Attend
Schools over 500

	Public	Catholic
Raw difference	63	
Parental income	56	
Parental education	51	
Parental college pland	42	
Learning environment	41	
College plans of student in 8th grade	39	
Use of time	38	
Religious order	28	
Discipline	22	13*
Quality of instruction	13*	16

*No longer significant

twice as important as discipline in accounting for the remaining Catholic school effect after all prior factors are taken into account.

The same finding can be viewed differently (Table 6.9), where the relative impact of religious order, discipline, and instruction on academic performance for students in schools with an enrollment of more than 500 is presented. Religious order ownership and discipline make their contributions, but neither is as important as the quality of academic instruction.

Otis Dudley Duncan suggested to me that one might also find it useful to vary the denominational affiliation of black students. Duncan observed that parental choice of a Catholic school would involve an even more decisive exercise of an option by a non-Catholic black parent than it would by a Catholic black parent. Therefore, one would expect a substantially larger difference—if the parental choice explanation were totally valid—between public school and Catholic school

TABLE 6.9
**Relationship between Religious Order Ownership, Discipline, and Quality of
Instruction as Correlates of Academic Performance for Minority Students
(Schools with More Than 500 Students)**

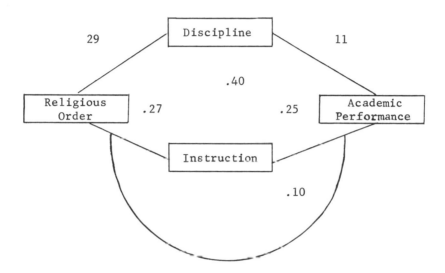

non-Catholic blacks than one would find between public school and
Catholic school Catholic blacks. As Table 6.10 illustrates, the differences are minimal. Non-Catholic blacks in Catholic schools are 52
standardized points above their counterparts in public schools while
Catholic blacks are 48 points ahead of their counterparts. When social
class differences between the two groups are taken into account, the
magnitude of the difference is not affected. Parental choice of a Catholic school for a non-Catholic black may be more momentous but contributes little to academic achievement. Our explanation then tilts a
little more in the direction of a school effect explanation.

College aspiration differences seem to be accounted for by an explanation which relies only on student background and are sufficient to
account for the differences between blacks and Hispanics who go to
Catholic schools and blacks and Hispanics who go to public schools.

TABLE 6.10
Academic Performance of Blacks in Catholic Schools and Public Schools by Religion
(Z Score)

	Black Catholics	Black Non-Catholics
Raw difference between public and Catholic school students	48	52
Difference net of social class	35	39

For homework differences and especially academic performance differences, there is considerable reason to tilt in the direction of a school effect explanation. The evidence can be summed up in the following propositions:

1. When background characteristics are held constant, there remains a substantial difference in scores between public school and Catholic school minority young people. This difference can be eliminated if one takes into account such school environment dimensions as ownership by a religious order, disciplinary control, and the quality of instructional experience.
2. Religious order ownership is not an aspect of either parental choice or family background.
3. While disciplinary control and academic quality can in part be accounted for also by a background characteristic explanation (as we have seen in prior chapters), some of the academic quality and disciplinary effect of Catholic schools seemed to be not the result of differences in perception based on different student backgrounds but on objective differences in the schools.
4. When one varies a structural aspect of an educational institution which is not likely to be the object of parental choice—in this case, the size of the school—one increases or diminishes the educational effect.
5. When one varies denominational affiliation, one finds that black non-Catholics do not disproportionately benefit from attending Catholic schools. Even the parental choice in their case involves opting not merely for a private school but for a private school of a different religious denomination. Thus the probability of a school effect over a parental choice effect is enhanced by the fact that those whose parents must make a more diffi-

cult choice do not thereby gain any extra academic performance advantage.

We lean in the direction of the following explanation. Young people with minority group backgrounds who attend Catholic schools study more and score higher on academic achievement tests in part because they come from very different family backgrounds and have very different personal characteristics. But they all study more and do better in tests in part because of the superior quality of Catholic schools—the result of religious order ownership, disciplinary effectiveness, and the quality of academic instruction. Of the three school environment dynamics which seem to contribute to the superior performance of black and Hispanic students in Catholic schools, the most important is the apparent superior quality of academic instruction in these schools— even when the other two environmental factors are held constant.

7.

Catholic Secondary Schools and Upward Mobility

It is often assumed in discussion among educators that one of the reasons for the apparent success of Catholic secondary schools is that they are especially likely to attract the children of the ambitious and upwardly mobile minority group families and hence have the "cream" of the educationally motivated members of such communities. Would not, it is often asked, such young people do well in any academic environment? If one compares the powerfully motivated young people in Catholic and public schools will they not both do equally well? Is not the apparent success of Catholic schools due to the disproportionate number of such strongly motivated young people in Catholic schools?

In this chapter we will explore that possibility and discover that the opposite is the case: the biggest difference between Catholic and public secondary school students among minorities is found in the upwardly mobile group. Hence the tilt in the direction of a school effect explanation increases.

The past several chapters have assumed that the correlation between social-class variables and academic performance for minority young people is the same in both the public and Catholic school groups. It is possible, however, that the model in the previous chapter has been

TABLE 7.1
Correlations for Minority Students between Academic Performance and Social Class by School Type

API with	Public	Catholic
Income	.21	.08
Father's education	.17	.09
Mother's education	.13	.00

"misspecified," that is, that there are different correlations between social class and success for the two groups—with the correlations stronger for the Catholic school students, since parental choice presumably would heighten the strength of the relationship between social class and academic outcome.

In fact, however (Table 7.1), just the opposite is the case: correlations between social class and achievement are much lower among Catholic school students. The educational effectiveness of Catholic schools is more evenly distributed among social-class groups than is the effectiveness of public schools.

Interaction "terms" were constructed for each of the three social-class variables (there was no difference between the two groups in the correlation between parental expectation of college graduation and academic performance). Two of the interaction terms were statistically significant, both of them for parental education. (An interaction term is the product of parental education multiplied by the "Catholic" dummy variable.)

Statistically speaking, it is inevitable that when these interaction terms are added to the model, the power of the social-class variables to diminish the difference between Catholic and public school minority students will be eroded. The effect of these two terms in the model is dramatic. They increase the difference between the two groups in academic performance to 96 standardized points, almost a full standard deviation. The likelihood of a family background explanation is notably diminished by such a phenomenon.

The notion of interaction terms and an increase in the difference between the two groups may be difficult for the reader who is not a

TABLE 7.2
Academic Performance for Minorities by Father's Education and School Type
(Z Score)

	Public	Catholic
Father did not attend college	.76	-25
Father did attend college	-.12	01

statistician to comprehend. The same finding can be demonstrated in another way which will also illustrate the impact of Catholic secondary schools on the children of upwardly mobile families (defined as those who did not attend college but expect a college graduation for their child).

Contrary to what one might have expected from the previous discussion of the impact of Catholic secondary schools, they are only marginally more successful with young people whose father attended college (Table 7.2). But 13 standardized points separate these two groups. Their greatest success is concentrated among the minority students whose fathers did not attend college. Here the difference between the two groups is 51 standardized points.

This difference seems to be concentrated among those whose fathers did not go to college but who are expected by their parents to be college graduates (the comparison in the last two figures in the top row of Table 7.3). Instead of these presumably powerfully motivated young people doing equally well no matter where they go to high school, they

TABLE 7.3
Expectation of Parent for Child
(Z Score)

	Not college graduate		College graduate	
	Public	Catholic	Public	Catholic
Father did not attend college	-79	-63	-57	-10
Attended college	-42	-29	11	04

represent the group with the biggest single difference (even after by definition parental education and aspiration have been accounted for) between students in public schools and Catholic schools.

It is hard to escape the conclusion that it is among the upwardly mobile—those with the best chance of creating a new black and Hispanic professional upper middle class—that Catholic schools are most successful. Another way of looking at the same phenomenon is to compare the difference between the first and third numbers in Table 7.3, row one, and the second and fourth numbers. An additional increment from parental college expectations for their child in those families where the father did not attend college is 22 standardized points in public schools and 53 standardized points in Catholic schools. If you did not go to college but expect your child to be a college graduate, a Catholic secondary school education seems to be a wise investment.

The difference between public and Catholic upwardly mobiles can be reduced to statistical insignificance (Table 7.4) almost entirely by school effect variables—order ownership, disciplinary environment, and quality of teaching. Discipline seems to be somewhat more important for this group (Table 7.5) than it is for the rest of the population—

TABLE 7.4
Model to Explain Difference for Upwardly Mobile Minority Group Members*
(Z Score)

Raw difference	47
Learning environment	47
College plans in 8th grade	42
Use of time	41
Order ownership	37
Discipline	20
Quality of instruction	17**

*Those whose fathers did not attend college but who are themselves expected to attend college

**Not significant

TABLE 7.5
**Relationship between Religious Order Discipline and Instructional Quality for
Upwardly Mobile Minority Members**

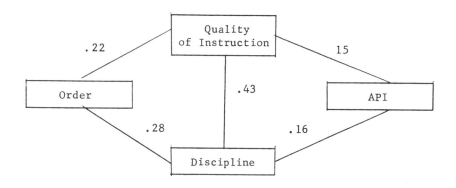

it is about as important as quality of instruction (and not less important) when the two are considered together.

It would appear then that Catholic secondary schools are particularly successful in the education of black and Hispanic young people from a lower social-class background. It is legitimate to wonder whether the reason for this might be that these schools were initially established—for the most part between 1910 and 1960—to educate the children of the immigrant class and prepare them for upward mobility. If such is the case, the apparent success of Catholic high schools with poor blacks and Hispanics would have less to do with race and more with social class: Catholic schools have their seeming success with blacks and Hispanics because they are geared to work with the upwardly mobile "poor."

One way to explore this possibility is to ask whether Catholic schools even today have a similar impact on lower social-class whites than on blacks and Hispanics. The evidence here suggests that this is the case. Thirty-seven standardized points separate public school whites from noncollege educated families and Catholic school whites (almost entirely Catholic in religion) from similar background. Discipline and quality of instruction seem to play the same role for the educational achievement of "poor" whites as they do for "poor" blacks and Hispanics (Tables 7.6 and 7.7). Catholic schools seem then

TABLE 7.6
Model to Explain Difference in Academic Achievement for Whites from Noncollege Backgrounds in Catholic and Public Secondary Schools (Z Score)

Raw difference	38
Parental college expectation for student	20
Learning environment in home	17
Discipline in school	11
Quality of instruction	00

TABLE 7.7
Relative Influence of Quality of Instruction and Discipline for Whites Whose Father Did Not Go to College

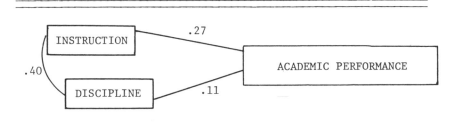

TABLE 7.8
Correlation between Social Class and Academic Performance for Catholic School and Public School Whites

	Public	Catholic
Income	.12	.09
Father's education	.23	.09
Mother's education	.24	.10

TABLE 7.9
Academic Performance by Father's College Attendance for Whites

	Public	Catholic
Father did not go to college	-05	25
Father went to college	43	47

to have their apparent success as "ethnic" institutions, though now new ethnic immigrant groups seem to be benefiting from them.

The case for a school effect is not absolutely conclusive yet. Still, the apparent success of Catholic schools cannot be explained any longer by the argument that they get the best motivated students. For it now seems that it is precisely among the best motivated students where the Catholic schools produce the most striking educational outcome differences.

The educational effectiveness of Catholic schools then seems less dependent on the social-class background of students. High academic performance scores were more evenly distributed among students of differing social-class background. This finding is so unusual in educational research that it is worth asking whether it only applies to minority students or to all who attend Catholic high schools. Table 7.8 indicates that the lower correlations between social class and achievement are true for whites who attend Catholic schools as well as minority group members.

The same finding can be seen in Table 7.9. In public schools 48 standardized points separate the achievement scores of those whose fathers went to college from those whose fathers did not. In the Catholic schools, however, only 20 points separate the two social-class groups.

If this is really a Catholic school phenomenon, one would expect the difference to narrow for both white and black students who are seniors. This is precisely what happens (Table 7.10). Approximately three-

TABLE 7.10
Differences between Two Social-Class Groups in Academic Achievement Scores
by Grades and Race
(Z Score)

	Sophomore	Senior
Public (White)	56	42
Catholic (White)	33	13
Public (Non-white)	54	33
Catholic (Non-white)	29	17

tenths of a standard deviation separates the college father families from the noncollege father families in the achievement tests of Catholic school sophomores (regardless of race), while 13 points separate the two groups among whites and 17 points among nonwhites. By the senior year, Catholic high schools have virtually equalized the performance of both social-class groups (regardless of race) while two-fifths of a standard deviation still separates the white students in public schools in the two social-class groups and one-third of a standard deviation still separates the nonwhites in the two social classes.

Differences between social classes in achievement scores will narrow in part between sophomore and senior years because there will be more dropouts, presumably, among the less affluent. Coleman *(Private and Public Schools)* has shown that the 24 percent sophomore/senior dropout rate of the public schools is twice the 12 percent dropout rate in Catholic schools. Thus the dropout rate theoretically ought to serve to narrow the differences between social-class groups even more in public schools than in Catholic schools. Coleman shows that when the dropout rate is taken into account one can create models which show greater improvement in test scores between sophomore and senior years in Catholic schools. However, one cannot estimate the dropout rates by social-class background with Coleman's models and hence one must wait for senior test data on the actual sophomores in the High School & Beyond sample. It is reasonable to assume that such data will show gaps between the two social-class groups in public schools that are only slightly different from the sophomore gaps. Thus the relative decline of the disadvantage of lower-class nonwhites in public schools in Table 7.10 is almost certainly a function of their higher dropout rate. One would be on reasonably safe ground in suspecting that when dropout rates are taken into account the 42-point difference between lower-class and upper-class white seniors in public schools will be the minimum class difference measured when data become available on present sophomores in their senior year. Thus the Catholic school impact of diminishing social-class differences will certainly not be attenuated when dropouts are taken into account and will probably be strengthened. Coleman's finding about superior learning rates in the sophomore/senior comparison for Catholic schools is another bit of evidence tilting in the direction of Catholic school effect.

Another way of viewing the matter is to look at the correlations between parental social class and academic performance in the sophomore and senior year in both Catholic and public schools (Table 7.10A). In public schools the correlations do not diminish. In Catholic schools the correlations between social class and achievement diminish from .28 in the sophomore year to .11 in the senior year, and for minority students from .16 in the sophomore year to .08 (statistically insignificant) in the senior year. The correlation coefficient between social class and achievement are not strikingly different in Catholic and public schools in the sophomore year, but by the senior year the correlation between social class and achievement is three times stronger in public schools than in Catholic schools. It would appear that the educational process in Catholic schools between the sophomore and senior years contributes substantially to an equalization of academic payoff among students regardless of their social-class background. This phenomenon tilts our pointer even more in the direction of a school effect outcome. Of course, it does not prove such an outcome definitively. Note also in Table 7.10B that while the differences between blacks and whites increase somewhat between the sophomore and senior years in public schools (despite the heavy attrition of black students), the differences diminish somewhat in Catholic schools. Minority seniors in Catholic schools have higher achievement scores than white sophomores in public schools and are only a quarter of a stan-

TABLE 7.10A
**Correlations between Father's Education and Academic Achievement in
Catholic and Public Schools and for Minority Students by Grade**

	Catholic		Public	
	Sophomore	Senior	Sophomore	Senior
All students	.28	.11	.33	.31
Minority students	.16	.08*	.23	.26

*Not statistically significant

dard deviation behind white seniors in public schools (who are four-fifths of a standard deviation ahead of their own minority counterparts).

The same phenomenon is not duplicated in non-Catholic private schools. The correlations with social class for academic performance are, if anything, higher than in public schools (Table 7.11) and there are 68 points difference between those from the two social-class groups.

There is four-fifths of a standard deviation in academic achievement scores between the two social-class groups among sophomores and half a standard deviation among seniors. One cannot argue that private schools attract a kind of student from a noncollege family who will do just as well academically as a student from a college family. On the contrary, it would appear that either Catholic schools alone attract a student from a noncollege family who has remarkable ability and/or

TABLE 7.10B
**Academic Achievement Scores for White and Minority Students in Catholic
and Public Schools by Grade**

	White		Minority	
	Catholic	Public	Catholic	Public
Sophomore	.15	-.17	-.46	-.88
Senior	.49	.20	-.07	-.59

TABLE 7.11
**Correlations between Academic Performance and Social Class for
Non-Catholic Private Schools**

Income	.32
Mother's education	.41
Father's education	.34

motivation or that there is a unique Catholic school effect. The fact
that the differences descend to virtual insignificance among seniors in
Catholic schools and not in either public or "other" private schools
tilts the explanation in the latter direction (Table 7.12).

The capacity to educate effectively the children of the noncollege
educated seems to exist in Catholic schools regardless of racial or linguistic background, perhaps a holdover from the days when Catholic
high schools were the path of upward mobility for ethnic immigrants.
It may be precisely the immigrant background that gives Catholic secondary schools the ability to deal with the problem of the children of
ambitious families who did not attend college themselves. The largest
difference between Catholic and public school students, when parental
aspirations and educational background are held constant, is precisely
among the upwardly mobile (Table 7.13).

On the other hand (in the bottom row of Table 7.13), Catholic
schools are less successful than public schools (hence the minus differ-

TABLE 7.12
**Academic Performance by Father's Education for Non-Catholic Private
Schools
(Z Score)**

Father went to college	91
Father did not go to college	23

TABLE 7.13
Academic Achievement by Father's Education and Parental College Plans for
Respondent by School Attended
(All Respondents)
(Z Score)

		Public	Catholic	Difference
Do not plan college graduation	Father did not attend college	-51	-31	20
	Father did attend college	-13	02	15
Do plan college graduation	Father did not attend college	00	21	21
	Father did attend college	51	38	-13

ence sign) in educating the graduation-bound children of college attenders. In an astonishing turn of the tables, it would appear that instead of the public schools being the great assimilators, they are most successful with the affluent while Catholic schools are most successful with the poor (if parental education can be taken as a surrogate of affluence and poverty). Their success with the black and Hispanic poor is but a reflection of a larger success in breaking social-class barriers to achievement. Presumably the public schools which the offspring of ambitious, college-educated families attend are very different from those which the children of the noncollege educated attend.

Any one of the three school characteristic variables we have been using can account for the difference in academic achievement between upwardly mobile Catholic and public school students (Table 7.14), though the quality of instruction is clearly the most important. Indeed (Table 7.15), if the academic achievement score is standardized only for quality of instruction, the differences between Catholic and public school students in the various parental education/parental aspiration categories are reduced to triviality, save in the case of the college bound from college-educated families where the difference is somewhat increased (Table 7.16).

Catholic schools are able to facilitate the upward mobility of the poor, especially if they are ambitious, because children of such families find the quality of instruction better in Catholic schools. However,

TABLE 7.14
**Model to Explain the Difference between Catholic and Public School
Achievement for Students from Families in Which Father Did Not Go to
College But Student is Expected to Graduate from College
(Z Score)**

Raw difference	21
Order ownership	16
Discipline	06
Quality of instruction	02[*]

[*]Not significant

the children of the well educated who themselves are college bound do somewhat less well in Catholic schools.

There are, as Peter Rossi would say, a number of ironies in the fire: (1) Catholic schools are apparently more effective at eliminating social inequality than public schools. (2) The Catholic population is rapidly

TABLE 7.15
**Academic Achievement, Order Ownership, Quality of Instruction, and
Discipline for Those from Families in Which Father Did Not Go to College But
Student Is Expected to Graduate from College**

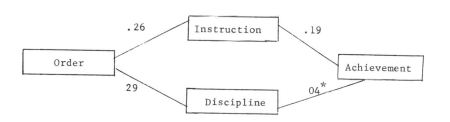

TABLE 7.16
**Academic Achievement by Father's Education and Parental College Plans by
School Attended with Achievement Standardized for Quality of Instruction**

		Public	Catholic	Difference
Do not plan college graduation	Father did not attend college	-51	-20	02
	Father did attend college	-13	09	-07
Do plan college graduation	Father did not attend college	00	24	02
	Father did attend college	51	39	-23

moving into a category where its own schools will be less effective for them than public schools.

Obviously much more research is required before these findings can be thought to be anything but highly tentative. However, the noncorrelation between social class and academic outcome in Catholic schools surely deserves more research.

Catholic schools seem less successful in producing high academic scores for young people who are college bound from college-educated families. Two factors seem to determine this phenomenon—size of school and religious order ownership (Table 7.17). Catholic schools do as well as public schools if they enroll more than 1,000 students or if they were owned by religious orders. The smaller diocesan-owned high schools do not seem to be able to provide such an effective challenge to their students from well-educated backgrounds who are destined for college, perhaps because dioceses do not have a tradition of academic excellence such as religious orders (or some religious orders) maintain. More than half (53 percent) of the Catholic white students in Catholic secondary schools are children of college educated fathers.

In conclusion, the apparent effect of Catholic schools discussed in this book seems to be as true of lower-class whites as it is of lower-class minority students. The effect of Catholic schools seems to be to diminish the impact of social class on academic achievement and virtually eliminate this difference by the time the students are seniors in high school. Our explanatory model understates the likelihood of a school effect because it assumes the same correlation between social

TABLE 7.17
**Academic Performance of Students Whose Father Went to College and Whose
Parents Plan That They Graduate from College**
(Z Score)

	Less than 1,000 Students	More than 1,000 Students
Public schools	62	47
Catholic schools:		
Owned by religious order	52	49
Now owned by religious order	18	45

class and achievement in both kinds of schools, whereas in fact the correlation is lower to nonexistent in Catholic schools. When an interaction term which takes this fact into account is entered into the model, the magnitude of the Catholic school impact increases instead of decreases.

It would appear that the Catholic school effect is "ethnic" and "social class" rather than specifically racial. These schools were established in great part to facilitate the upward mobility of European ethnic immigrant groups. In ways which need to be determined further but which relate to both style of discipline and quality of instruction, these schools have been especially successful with upwardly mobile "ethnic immigrants" and still are, whether the "ethnics" be black, brown, or white. Far from the success of the schools being explained by their selectively attracting the upwardly mobile, the effect seems to be specifically occurring in that group, since the biggest difference between Catholic and public secondary schools is found precisely in this group where achievement motivation can safely be presumed to be the highest both in the student and the family.

There is an irony in this apparent success, however; Catholic schools are only barely comparable to public schools in their impact on young people from college-educated families (many of whom, it is safe to assume, are children of earlier generations of Catholic school attenders whose rise to the college class was facilitated by Catholic school attendance). The Catholic secondary school does very well indeed with those population groups from which the church's membership tends to be moving and much less well (only barely adequately) with those population groups into which the church's membership has been moving.

It would appear that there is a classic case of culture lag at work. Institutionally, Catholic secondary education is unaware of the change in social class of its primary clientele (a phenomenon which has only emerged a couple of decades ago). It continues to do well what it always did well, much to the benefit of newer upwardly mobile (often non-Catholic) students. It remains to be seen whether Catholic high schools can minister successfully to the needs of the urban poor and the suburban middle class in years to come.

The certainty of a Catholic school effect is not established by this chapter. However, the power of the tilt in that direction is enhanced by the finding that Catholic schools seem to eliminate by the time a student is a senior the effect of parental social class on academic achievement, a finding as rare in educational research as it is striking.

8.

Effect of Academic Tracking

Catholic high schools are often reputed to be college preparatory and as Table 8.1 clearly indicates, both white and minority students are approximately twice as likely to be in academic programs if they attend Catholic schools. It is therefore possible that the assignment of a child in the Catholic school to an academic track, either based on the young person's previous academic performance or on the orientation of the school, might affect differential educational outcomes of Catholic and public schools, particularly of minority students. In this chapter we will investigate the effects of the different tracking programs in Catholic and public schools and consider a serious charge leveled at an earlier draft of this report by the staff of the National Center for Education Statistics.

If the effect of Catholic schools is based on a preselection of students who are either oriented toward or prepared for a college track, then one would expect the differences between Catholic and public schools to be eliminated when students in academic programs of Catholic schools are compared with students in academic programs of public schools, and when students in general programs of Catholics schools are compared to students in general programs of public schools. However, academic tracking does not explain the differences between Catholic and public schools, but rather specifies the differences, both for minority and white students (Table 8.2). The differences between students in

TABLE 8.1
Proportion in Academic Tracks in Catholic and Public Schools by Group

	Catholic	Public
White	65%	36%
Minority	64%	29%

academic tracks in Catholic and public schools are virtually nonexistent if the students are white, and decline to 30 standardized points if the students are minority. Substantial differences remain (for minority students 34 standardized points for those in general programs, and for white students 19 points for those in general programs) for students who are not in academic tracks. If the minority student is sufficiently motivated or prepared to obtain admission into an academic track, it makes relatively little difference whether that student goes to a Catholic or public school compared to the difference it has made for those who are in general programs. The special Catholic school effect seems to be concentrated among those who are not well enough prepared or not sufficiently motivated to obtain admission into the academic track.

If the Catholic school effect is to be found especially among those who were on the general track, one would anticipate that the changes

TABLE 8.2
API by Track for Groups in Catholic and Public Schools

	Minority		White	
	Catholic	Public	Catholic	Public
General	−50	−84	−07	−26
Academic	−07	−20	56	59
Other	−88	−109	−22	−42
Total	−24	−74	32	02

TABLE 8.3
Academic Achievement by Grade, Track and Race for Catholic and Public
School Students
(API—Z Score)

| | Minority | | | | | | White | | | | | |
| | Catholic | | | Public | | | Catholic | | | Public | | |
	Soph.	Sen.	Change	Soph.	Sen.	Change	Soph.	Sen.	Change	Soph.	Sen.	Change
Academic	−31	13	+44	−48	03	+51	40	70	+30	39	79	+40
General	−58	−39	+19	−87	−82	+05	−20	12	+32	−42	−05	+36
Other	−112	−68	+44	−125	−94	+31	−40	−12	+28	−65	−25	+40

between sophomore and senior year for students in the general program, especially for minority students, will be greater than for students in public schools. Table 8.3 confirms this expectation. General track minority students who are seniors in Catholic schools are 19 points higher on the standardized tests than are sophomores; whereas public school seniors are only 5 points higher on the tests than sophomores. To look at the matter from a different perspective (Table 8.4), the differences between Catholic and public school minority students in the academic tracks diminish from 17 to 10 points between the sophomore and senior year; whereas the difference between those in the general track increases from 29 standardized points to 43.

Although Catholic schools are twice as likely to place minority students in academic tracks, it turns out that the most notable effect of Catholic schools is not on those in the academic track but on those in the general track, and this effect seems to increase between the sophomore and the senior years. This effect seems especially likely to occur for those minority students whose fathers did not attend college and who are in the general track (Table 8.5). There is only a slight difference between Catholic and public minority students in the general track whose fathers did attend college, but 26 standardized points difference between the two groups in the general track if the father did not attend college (the same phenomenon is found among white general track students). The apparent Catholic school effect is concentrated on the multiply disadvantaged students: students who come from a background of low educational achievement by the parents, and whose own educational achievement does not permit them to obtain entrance into an academic track. Far from the effect of Catholic schools being ex-

TABLE 8.4
Difference in Academic Achievement Scores between Public and Catholic
School Students by Race, Track, and Grade
(Z Score Advantage of Catholic)

	Minority		White	
	Sophomore	Senior	Sophomore	Senior
Academic	17	10	01	−09
General	29	43	22	18
Other	13	26	25	13

plained by the fact that Catholic schools require better motivated students from better educated families (a charge repeated often by critics of the present research in the preliminary report—apparently without having read it), the opposite seems to be the case. The Catholic school effect seems to be especially concentrated among those whose family educational background and own educational experience do not incline them toward achievement.

We noted in chapter 7 that there is an "interaction" between father's educational attainment and Catholic school attendance. There is a lower correlation between father's educational achievement and academic performance for those who attend Catholic schools. There is also, as shown in this chapter, a lower correlation between academic

TABLE 8.5
Academic Performance for Students in General Track by Father's Education,
School Attended, and Minority Status
(Z Score)

	Minority			White		
	Cath.	Pub.	Dif.	Cath.	Pub.	Dif.
Father did not attend college	−56	−82	26	−06	−30	24
Father attended college	−25	−29	04	−05	−08	03

tracking and educational performance for those who attend Catholic schools. The impact of these two interactions can be studied in Table 8.6. The difference between Catholic and public school students, whether they be white or minority, diminishes when one takes into account father's educational achievement, but if the interaction effect is added to the model, the difference between Catholic and public school minority and white students increases dramatically. Adding to the model the educational track in which the student has been placed, the difference again diminishes. But when the interaction term between academic track and Catholic school is considered, the difference returns to its original half a standard deviation between public and Catholic school students.

For those unfamiliar with the use of interaction terms in multiple regression models, it should be added that Table 8.6 adds nothing to the findings already presented in this chapter, but merely states them in a different fashion: even though minority students in Catholic schools are more likely to come from well-educated families and more likely to be placed in academic tracks, neither of these phenomena account for the difference between the performance of minority students in Catholic schools and those in public schools. As we saw in the last chapter, there is virtually no correlation between education of parents and achievement for Catholic school students, and a much smaller correlation between tracking and achievement for Catholic school students. The educational experience of one's parent and the academic track in

TABLE 8.6
Model for Academic Performance, Tracking, Father's Education, and Interactions
(Z Score)

	Minority	White
Raw difference between Catholic and public	49	32
Father's education	42	23
Interaction between education and Catholic	69	65
Education track	21	33
Interaction between track and Catholic	48	37

which one has been placed are less important in Catholic schools for both minority and white students than they are in public schools.

Yet another way of making the point of this chapter is presented in Table 8.7. Thirty-three standardized points separate the academic performance of general track students in Catholic schools from that of general track students in public schools when both sets of students come from families whose fathers did not go to college. If one adds the two motivational factors of parental college aspirations and student college aspirations, the difference is reduced by 25 standardized points. Adding the two school effect factors—quality of teaching and school discipline—the difference is reduced to statistical insignificance. In other words, about a quarter of the raw difference between academic track in noncollege family Catholic and public school students can be accounted for by the motivational variables of parental and student college aspirations. The rest of the difference is eliminated when one takes into account the quality of teaching and the disciplinary environment in the school. It cannot be argued conclusively from this analysis that there is beyond all doubt a Catholic school effect, but one can point out that a difference between Catholic school minority students and public school minority students seems to be concentrated among the multiply disadvantaged and cannot be accounted for by the superior educational background of parents or by superior educational performance of the student which has won him/her admission to an academic track. The advantage the multiply disadvantaged minority student seems to experience in Catholic schools can be accounted for in substantial part by the student's own evaluation of the quality of instruction and the disciplinary environment. These findings require further investigation of what goes on in Catholic school classrooms and why they seem especially able to determine who are, by virtue of family background, educational background, and their own academic skills, not likely to perform well in secondary schools.

The National Center for Education Statistics, under severe pressure from congressional and bureaucratic opponents of private schools, issued a hasty critique of this report before a public seminar at which preliminary findings of the report were to be presented. This critique— unethical in both its haste and its failure to consider responses from the author of the report—argued that when a model at NCES was used, the differences between Catholic and public school students vanished and that therefore the present was thoroughly discredited. In Table 8.8, the

TABLE 8.7

Model Explaining Differences between Catholic and Public School Minority Students Whose Fathers Did Not Go to College and Who Are Not in the Academic Track in Their Schools

	Z Score
Raw difference	33
Parental college aspiration	25
Students' college aspiration in 8th grade	25
Quality of teaching index	17
School discipline index	10*

*Difference no longer statistically significant

standardized correlation coefficients (betas) of the NCES model are presented for sophomores and seniors, along with the standardized correlation coefficients obtained when the NCES model is rerun, taking into account the two interaction terms discussed in this chapter. When the interaction terms are taken into account, the coefficient for "Catholic" is statistically significant in both sophomore and senior years and is .24 higher than that of the NCES model in the senior year.

There was no excuse for the failure of the NCES staff to take into account the interaction coefficient (save for the possibility that they did not understand what an interaction term was), for the text of the report indicates the existence of statistically significant interaction in the analysis. To deliberately leave these terms out of their critique leaves NCES open to the charge of either unethical or incompetent behavior and quite possibly both. Their critique reduced the correlation between Catholic and academic performance to statistical insignificance. When, in fact, the interaction terms were added to the model the Catholic correlation became not only significant, but for seniors stronger than both SES and mother's college expectation. The NCES criticism "covered up"—deliberately or not—the principal finding of this report. It undoubtedly won for NCES some immunity from pressure from the educational establishment and from congressional critics, but it ought not to win for them any respect for their professional competence or integrity.

TABLE 8.8
Effect of Interaction Terms on NCES Reanalysis—Correlation Coefficients (r)

	Sophomores		Seniors	
	NCES Model	NORC Model*	NCES Model	NORC Model*
SES**	.18	.17	.15	.19
Program	.25	.37	.32	.32
Mother's expectation	.20	.20	.21	.21
Race***	.25	.26	.27	.32
Sex	−.07	−.05	.07	.03
Catholic	.00	.09	−.01	.23

*Two interaction terms included: 1) Father's education by Catholic
                              2) Program by Catholic
**Father's education in NORC Model
***White vs. Black and Hispanic.

The college orientation of Catholic high schools in no sense can be to account for the differences between minority students in those schools and in other schools. Quite the contrary; Catholic schools seem to have their most notable effect on those students who are not in the college-oriented track and their most powerful effect on multiply disadvantaged students—members of minority groups whose fathers did not attend college and who themselves are not sufficiently equipped in educational experience to be admitted to academic track programs. Not only is the correlation between social class and educational achievement nonexistent in Catholic schools, but the correlation between academic tracking and educational performance is substantially lower in Catholic schools than it is in public schools. When these two interactions are taken into account, it becomes evident that neither family educational background nor previous educational experience of the student is sufficient to account for the Catholic school effect on minorities.

9.

Finances of Catholic Schools

If the school effect of Catholic secondary education toward which we have tilted in the previous chapter is confirmed by further research, one will have to submit that Catholic secondary education is one of the best bargains, particularly for minority students, ever offered in the educational marketplace. As we shall demonstrate in this chapter, Catholic schools operate with a per pupil cost approximately half of that of public schools and charge tuition that is less than half of that of other private schools. Even though they have very little in the way of subsidies and almost no government assistance, Catholic schools accomplish their effects (such as these may be) at bargain basement prices for reasons that cannot be explained away by lower faculty salaries, inferior faculty qualifications, or higher ratios of students to teachers.

In the analysis in this chapter we will turn from data files recording the responses of students in the High School and Beyond study to the file recording the responses of principals describing their institutions. Table 9.1 shows the distribution of schools from which principals submitted responses: 746 public schools, 35 non-Catholic private schools, and 82 Catholic schools. Catholic schools are smaller than public schools, indeed on the average only half as large (Table 9.2), they have less library books, are more likely to be nonunion, employ teachers who are more likely to leave the faculty and less likely to survive on it for ten years, and marginally less likely to have an M.A. or a Ph.D. (Table 9.2). However, their dropout rate is almost nonexistent. Three-quarters of their graduates (according to the principals) are enrolled in college and their absentee rate among teachers is half that of public schools. Almost all of them accept non-Catholic students and they seem to have effective ratios of nonwhite students and nonwhite faculty (Table 9.2). In a fifth of the cases, a local school board appoints the principal; in two-fifths the religious order chooses the principal; and in another fifth a set of religious administrators (possibly the diocesan school superintendent) selects the principal. One-fifth of the schools have an independent board who selects the principals, a manifestation of the rapid democratization of Catholic education which has occurred—mostly unnoticed—since the Second Vatican Council. Religious order ownership is important in predicting educational outcome, but the orders own only a little less than two-fifths of the schools while half of them are owned by another religious organization, in all likelihood the diocese of the archdiocese. The difference in control and the different outcomes from such control merit further research. One has the impression that there is a tendency for a religious order to abandon control of the schools in which they teach. Unless some way can be

TABLE 9.1
Number of Schools

Public	707
Public alternative	39
Catholic	44
Black Catholic	30
Hispanic Catholic	8
Elite private	10
Other private	25

TABLE 9.2
School Characteristics

	Public	Catholic	Catholic Minority
Size	1,538	795	678
Library volumes	16,223	11,159	10,141
Non-union	13%	76%	77%
Drop-out rate last year	10.9	0.9	1.7
College attenders	44	75	78
Non-white students	28	11	64
Non-white faculty	14	5	16
Teachers:			
ten years	41	21	18
left last year	7	12	15
absentee rate of teachers (daily)	4	2	2
MA or Ph.D.	49	45	50
Accept non-Catholic		96	97

found to maintain the notable religious order impact we have reported in this volume, such policies may be a very serious mistake both for the religious order and for Catholic secondary education (Table 9.3).

There are also more students per faculty and staff in the Catholic school —one staff member for every eighteen students in a Catholic school as opposed to one for every fourteen students in a public school, and one for every seven in a special "alternative" public school. Other private schools also have one staff member for every seven students. In Catholic schools then there are three times as many students for each staff member as there are in private schools or special public schools and almost one-and-one-half times as many students per staff member as there are in ordinary public schools.

As might be expected from the college intentions described in earlier chapters, the graduates of these schools, according to the principals, are substantially more likely to go to college than the graduates of any of the public schools. The educational outcomes of the Catholic schools, described tentatively in previous chapters, are achieved de-

TABLE 9.3
(A) Who Appoints Principal (B) Ownership

	Catholic	Catholic Minority
Board	19	16
Order	43	51
Religious administrator	31	27
Other	7	5
B - OWNERSHIP		
School	5	0
Order	36	38
Other religious organization (Diocese)	50	54
Other	9	8

TABLE 9.4
Faculty and Staff Ratios
(Number of Students per Faculty and Staff)

	Staff	Faculty
Public	13.8	10.4
Public alternative	6.5	9.5
Catholic	18.9	13.2
Catholic black	17.9	12.8
Catholic hispanic	18.9	15.2
Elite private	7.5	6.3
Other private	6.3	4.3

TABLE 9.5
College Attendance Rate by School Type
(Percent of Last Graduation Class Enrolled in College)

Public	43
Public alternative	43
Catholic	76
Catholic black	78
Catholic hispanic	84
Elite private	99
Other private	71

spite the fact that there are more students per staff member, staff is more transient, and somewhat less likely to have an M.A. or Ph.D. There are no statistically significant correlations, however (Table 9.6), between staff ratio and college attendance, save in the opposite of the expected direction. The more students per faculty (or the less faculty

TABLE 9.6
Correlations between Staff Ratio and College Attendance
(The More Students per Faculty, the Higher the College Attendance Rate)

Public	.06
Public alternative	.27
Catholic	.01
Catholic minority	.12
Elite	-.01

TABLE 9.7
Percent M.A. or Ph.D. on Faculty

Public	49
Public alternative	61
Catholic	45
Catholic hispanic	46
Catholic black	50
Elite private	59
Other private	40

per students), the more likely are those who attend public alternative schools to go to college—almost as if the presence of too many staff members may impede college attendance. A faculty member who has more students for whom to be responsible apparently does not impede college attendance in either ordinary public or in Catholic schools.

In Catholic schools, costs (Table 9.8) are almost half that of public schools, substantially less than that of other private schools, and less than a third of the cost of elite private schools. Typical public school per-pupil cost is $1,807, elite private school costs per pupil are $3,598, other private schools are $1,508, and the typical Catholic high school is $1,097.

More than three-quarters of the funding of Catholic schools is raised through tuition (Table 9.9), and a subsidy (from a parish or diocese, presumably) accounts for approximately a tenth of the funding, and various "fund-raising" activities (bingo, raffles, etc., one imagines) account for another tenth. Government resources—federal, state, and local—contribute only 1 percent of the funding of Catholic schools. Whatever is to be said about such issues as vouchers, tuition tax credits, or parochial aid, it is evident that Catholic schools have not needed government support thus far to achieve remarkable effects, particularly with minority students.

TABLE 9.8
Per Pupil Cost for Various Schools

	Mean	STD
Public	1807	689
Public alternative	2218	677
Ordinary Catholic	1097	374
Catholic black	1139	489
Catholic hispanic	962	210
Elite private	3598	2503
Other private	1508	1583

Their tuition (Table 9.10) is under $900, less than half that of other private schools and less than a third that of elite private schools. Catholic schools achieve their apparent effect with smaller faculty, smaller budgets, and smaller charges. One would suppose that those interested in the economics of secondary education would be fascinated by the phenomenon.

Part of the explanation for all this is that Catholic schools pay their faculty members less, on the average almost $2,000 less for a beginning teacher with an A.B. (Table 9.11), although about a fifth of that difference can be attributed to the fact that there are less likely to be unions at Catholic secondary schools (Table 9.12). It may be that members of religious orders are willing to work for smaller salaries (at one time it might have been said that they almost had no choice, but it is very difficult in contemporary Catholic religious communities to force someone to do something she/he does not want to do). It may also be that some lay teachers on the faculties of such schools are motivated by religious or altruistic ideals, or find Catholic education a more congenial place in which to work, despite the poor salaries.

TABLE 9.9
Funding of Catholic Schools
(Percent)

	Ordinary	Minority
Tuition	74	79
Fund raising	9	7
Subsidy	11	9
Endowment	2	0
Other	3	4
Government	1	1
	100	100

There is no correlation between per-pupil cost and whether a school is owned by a religious order.

Can one account for the surprising difference in per-pupil costs between Catholic and public schools by taking into account the salaries, academic training of the staff, and the staff ratio in the school? Using the same kind of analytic model presented in previous chapters, but with the dependent variable now being the difference in per-pupil cost

TABLE 9.10
Tuition at Private Schools

	Mean	STD
Catholic	$ 857	$ 278
Black Catholic	839	196
Hispanic Catholic	855	162
Elite private	2,713	936
Other private	1,928	1,212

TABLE 9.11
Faculty Salary in Private Schools*

	Mean	STD
Public	$10,724	$1,189
Public alternative	10,792	676
Catholic	8,814	930
Catholic Black	8,730	657
Catholic Hispanic	8,184	1,163
Elite private	9,838	631
Other private	8,858	1,344

*Beginning teaching with B.A.

between all the Catholic and all the public schools in the survey, we can account for a little more than $200 of the differences in per-pupil costs between Catholic and public schools, most of it being attributable to different salary structures (salary structure here being measured by the beginning salary of a teacher with an A.B.). Catholic schools save some money because they pay their faculty less, they have fewer faculty members per student, and fewer M.A. and Ph.D. faculty. But most of the per-pupil cost savings of Catholic schools cannot be ac-

TABLE 9.12
Salary and Unions in Catholic Schools

Difference from public schools	$1,992
Difference net of union absence	$1,599

TABLE 9.13
Difference in per Pupil Costs between Catholic and Public Schools

Raw difference	$1,007
Net of salary	809
Net of degree	799
Net of staff ratio	791

counted for by such economy. The data available in the High School and Beyond research thus far does not enable us to go any further in why the costs of Catholic education are so low. The evidence suggests that Catholic secondary schools can do more—especially for minority students—at less cost. Minority parents who are sending their children to Catholic schools seem to be getting a good product for their money. Perhaps this is the reason why minority enrollment at such schools is apparently increasing. The marketplace, it seems, has had more interest in the quality of the product being offered in Catholic schools than has the education research community.

This chapter must necessarily end on a note of incompleteness. While we could only argue with some degree of probability from the preceding six chapters to a significant and important Catholic school educational effect, especially on minority young people, we can argue with near certainty on the basis of the present chapter that Catholic schools accomplish whatever they do accomplish at amazingly low costs. Those interested in educational costs might find this an irresistible conclusion.

Many people have suspected such a finding for some time, and there has been impressionistic evidence that strongly hinted that Catholic schools were remarkably efficient financially (one need only consider the tuition of Catholic schools and the annual budget for secondary education in various public school systems). Educational economists have not exactly broken down the doors of Catholic institutions in their efforts to discover where Catholic school administrators buy their mirrors.

10.

Conclusion

The evidence analyzed here tilts in the direction of the following explanation for the apparently superior performance of young people, especially minority group members, in Catholic schools. Some Catholic school effects are input effects. Young people who attend Catholic secondary schools are more likely to be confident of college graduation, not so much because of their Catholic school education as because they came to such schools with confidence of high school graduation and from families where educational expectations were strong.

Other special aspects of Catholic schools cannot be totally explained by the model applied here. The disciplinary control and academic excellence of Catholic schools are in part a result of the kinds of young people who choose or are chosen for these schools to begin with. But background factors cannot fully explain either the disciplinary or instructional excellence which appear to be characteristic of Catholic secondary schools.

Other Catholic school outcomes—more time spent on homework, higher academic test performance—are partially explained by input characteristics but are also partially explained by school effects, most notably by religious order ownership of the school, quality of discipline, and quality of teaching.

The success of Catholic secondary schools cannot be attributed to the fact that they are more likely to enroll students who come from upwardly mobile families and who are hence most likely to have powerful educational motivations. The opposite seems to be the case. The greatest differences between Catholic and public schools seems to be located among upwardly mobile young people. Motivation for success seems to be much more adequately rewarded with learning achievement in Catholic secondary schools than in public secondary schools.

Catholic schools may have some religious effect on Catholic students who attend them though the effect is modest. There is no evidence that Catholic schools have any religious effect on black and Hispanic students. The effect of Catholic schools seems to be especially powerful on the multiply disadvantaged—minority students whose parents did not attend college, who themselves have not qualified for academic programs. Thus the Catholic school effect cannot be explained or even reduced by taking into account the fact that Catholic schools selectively recruit from college-educated families and from students inclined toward academic programs. The success of Catholic schools with the multiply disadvantaged is the single most important finding in the present research and has been overlooked by most of those who rushed into newspaper print in criticism of the report, apparently without having read it carefully.

The Catholic school effects seem to be purchased at amazingly low cost. The schools support themselves mostly out of tuition, though tuition is approximately half of that paid in other private schools, and per-pupil cost is approximately $1,000 less than in public schools. The financial efficiency is accounted for only partially by higher student/teacher ratios, lower staff income, and lower rates of advanced-degree training for teachers in Catholic schools.

This is virtually the first study of Catholic secondary schools and minority students. It therefore constitutes at the most a preliminary approach to the educational interests involved. Some may feel that it raises more questions than it answers, but such is the nature of a preliminary investigation. Perhaps it more clearly specifies than has hitherto been done, the precise nature of the questions that must be asked in further research on Catholic education and in particular on Catholic secondary education.

1. Further attempts must be made to explore the possibility that the apparent Catholic school effects are indeed merely effects of parental choice and of the different family and personal characteristics of stu-

dents attending Catholic schools. Critics of this research or proponents of other research should specify what familial or student characteristics must be considered as possible explanations for the different outcomes of Catholic school attendance. Family size, father-absent families, education, income, parental college aspirations, learning environment, parental monitoring of homework, student's college plans when he/she entered high school, student's use of time, his/her psychological well-being, number of hours of TV watched—all these have already been taken into account. Those who believe it is necessary to maintain the tilt in the direction of a background explanation may no longer be content with vague references to family influence. They must specify what the nature of that influence is—unless it is the ineffable, in which case it is beyond empirical research and probably beyond discussion.

2. The influence of religious order impact must be investigated more closely. Religious order ownership sharply differentiates even within Catholic schools. The religious order has its influence on educational outcome in part because of its ability to maintain more disciplinary control and provide better quality instruction. But half of the religious order influence is not channeled through such intervening dynamics, nor can one say with any degree of confidence whether it is religious order faculty members who have the special effect or whether any faculty member in an environment influenced by a religious order is likely to be a more effective teacher and disciplinarian. There is a certain poignancy in the fact that many members of Catholic religious orders have lost confidence in their own work and membership in their religious communities is declining rapidly—precisely when educational research becomes available showing that religious orders apparently make a unique and important contribution to secondary education.

3. Since the more effective disciplinary control in Catholic schools cannot be explained by the background of their typical student, more research is needed on the reasons for such effect, especially the reasons why students themselves give Catholic schools such high marks on both disciplinary fairness and effectiveness. It is possible that Catholic schools are able to achieve this success because they do not admit or do not tolerate that numerically almost invisible segment of the student population who create serious problems in the disciplinary environment of the school. However, such an explanation is not automatically or inevitably true, and ought not be accepted without further investiga-

tion. Other dynamics may be at work and their location and specification ought to be of considerable interest to educational researchers if not to educational policymakers.

4. Attempts should be made to understand the reason for the very positive evaluation of the quality of instruction among students who attend Catholic secondary schools. The quality of instruction is the strongest correlate of academic outcome, and remains a very powerful predictor even when all background variables are taken into account. What goes on in the classroom does matter. The teacher's performance is important. We do not know the reason for the apparent success of classroom instructors in Catholic schools; the phenomenon requires further investigation. It has been proposed that in the continuation of the High School and Beyond project more detailed questions be asked on the instructional experience of students: what they define as effective teaching and what kinds of teaching behaviors seem typical of Catholic secondary schools and also correlate with academic achievement. Unfortunately there is at the present writing some possibility that such questions will be excluded from the questionnaire on the grounds that they are not proper (the reasons for the possible impropriety escape the present author).

5. The astonishing financial performance of Catholic schools ought to be studied. With little subsidy, less in the way of government help, and tuition rates half that of the typical private school, Catholic secondary schools seem not only to do as well as public schools but considerably better—even with the appropriate background variables held constant—in their educational effort. How do they accomplish their economies since one as a scientist must reject the possibility that they do it with mirrors?

At this late stage of educational research in the United States, it seems ironic to conclude by urging more research on Catholic secondary schools. They have been on the educational scene for a long time and there have been many hints, some of them merely anecdotal, on the findings reported in the present volume. The considerable number of non-Catholic blacks who send their children to Catholic school suggests that something interesting is occurring, yet there has been virtually no research. Proposals for the study of Catholic education on the grounds that it was an interesting and research-worthy aspect of the American educational enterprise have been routinely rejected by governmental and private funding agencies (in one case, by the National

Institutes for Education with the argument that such research should not be attempted because it might "redound to the credit of Catholic schools"). If one pretends a phenomenon is not there for a sufficiently long period of time, there is always the possibility that the phenomenon will go away. Such is the strategy reputed to be that of the ostrich.

One major question ought to be asked by the reader at the end of this report: Might there be something going on in the Catholic school, especially with regard to multiply disadvantaged students—minority students coming from a home background of low educational achievement who themselves are not able to be admitted to academic programs—that merits further investigation? The present report has not eliminated the possibility of a selectivity factor, but it has eliminated the possibility of the most obvious selectivity phenomena—parental and student aspiration, parental education, and student's previous academic performance. It has demonstrated that much of the difference that remains between Catholic and public school students when these other matters are taken into account can be explained in terms of the student's perception of the quality of classroom instruction and the disciplinary atmosphere of the school. Is it just possible that there might be something going on in the classrooms of Catholic schools from which other educational institutions in the country might learn?

Professor Diane Ravitch has remarked apropros of this question that it has been treated with "benign contempt." In the flurry of excitement which characterized the initial presentation of these findings in the spring of 1981, no one seems to have heard this question, much less bothered to respond to it. I am candidly at a loss as to understanding why, and therefore I conclude with an open letter to Dr. Ernest Boyer, former commissioner of education and president of the Carnegie Foundation for the Advancement of Teaching. The letter was occasioned by Dr. Boyer's dismissal of our research a few days after a preliminary presentation in Washington.

April 23, 1981

Dr. Ernest Boyer
The Carnegie Foundation
   for the Advancement of Teaching
437 Madison Avenue
New York, New York 10022

Dear Dr. Boyer:

It is altogether possible that you were misquoted in the *New York Times* article of Sunday, April 12, on the subject of the research done by James Coleman and me on Catholic schools. If indeed you were misquoted, then the rest of this letter is inoperative.

If, however, Ted Fiske quoted you correctly, I would ask if there is any other subject in the country, save Catholic schools, on which a man of your influence and importance would make such a fool of himself.

It takes scarcely five minutes of reading either of our reports to know that indeed the studies were based on national probability samples. I cannot believe that your statement to Mr. Fiske was based on anything more than a summary that someone else provided for you on the research findings.

May I call to your attention, should you be interested at all in the facts of the matter, that the fundamental findings which ought to have some pertinence to the Carnegie Foundation are that the payoff in attendance at Catholic schools for minority students is *not* for those from well-educated family backgrounds or who are academically promising (as would be judged by their presence in the academic track in their schools). On the contrary, the payoff for Catholic school attendance among minority young people comes precisely for those from relatively uneducated family background and who are in nonacademic tracks—those who are, in other words, thrice disadvantaged: by their racial background, their family educational background, and by their own prior educational achievement. If any other institutions in the country besides Catholic schools, Dr. Boyer, should produce such a phenomenon, would you be so quick to dismiss it as a result of a flaw in sampling design?

Since I can scarcely expect a man of your importance and obligations to read my report entirely, I append a single table [Table 8.7]. Without going into elaborate detail, the model shows that among the thrice disadvantaged—minority students whose fathers did not go to college and who are not in the academic track—there is a third of a standard deviation separating those in Catholic schools from those in public ones. When one takes into account both parental college aspirations and the students' own college aspirations, this difference is reduced by eight standardized points, so a quarter of a standard deviation remains. When one then further takes into account the quality of teaching in the schools as rated by the students themselves and the description of school discipline by the students themselves, the remaining difference is reduced to statistical insignificance. In other words, two-thirds of the explanatory power of the model can be attributed to school characteristics—discipline and teaching—while the other one-third of the explanatory power of the model can be attributed to familial and student ambition. The standardized coefficients for discipline and teaching are about the same: discipline net of teaching and teaching net of discipline have about the same effect.

I would not claim, Dr. Boyer, that this model (based on a national probability sample of students, incidentally) proves conclusively that there is a Catholic school effect, in part explained by the quality of teaching on the thrice disadvantaged. But I would suggest that there is enough evidence that this *may* be happening. If you tell me that the Carnegie Foundation for the Advancement of Teaching is not interested in the possibility that there may be a teaching factor at work in Catholic school which accounts for the superior performance of the thrice disadvantaged in those institutions, then I am forced to ask why a foundation concerned with the advancement of teaching is not interested in this possibility.

And if you tell me a priori that it is impossible that there be such an effect, again I would like to know the reason for such an assertion. Minimally, Coleman's research and mine suggest that the educational research establishment ought to take a closer look at what goes on in Catholic schools. I wonder why nobody has suggested this possibility. Or do you feel free, Dr. Boyer, to dismiss the work of a Catholic priest on the subject of Catholic schools as being so biased to begin with that it does not merit consideration?

I realize, as I have said previously, that you are very important and cannot be expected to read my report fully. However, I am making a presentation at the Lehrman Institute on May 8th and I am sure you could easily obtain an invitation to participate in the discussion. If you are not interested in learning more about the report, then once more I am forced back on my question: Why not?

Cordially yours,

Andrew M. Greeley
Senior Study Director, NORC
Professor of Sociology, University of Arizona

Dr. Boyer did not come to the presentation at the Lehrman Institute, nor did he ever acknowledge receipt of my letter of April 23.

APPENDIX

Hispanic Ethnic Groups

Catholic schools in the present study are much more likely to enroll Cuban students than public schools and considerably less likely to enroll Mexican-Americans (Table A1). Nevertheless, it is precisely among Mexican-Americans where the greatest difference in academic performance seems to occur: Catholic school Mexican-Americans are three-quarters of a standard deviation higher on the achievement tests than public school Mexican-Americans (Table A2).

TABLE A1
Spanish Ethnicity and Catholic School Enrollment
(Percent)

	Public	Catholic
Cuban	06	30
Mexican	61	39
Puerto Rican	11	17
Other	22	15

TABLE A2
API and Spanish Ethnic Groups

	Public Schools	Catholic Schools
Cuban	-25	+04
Mexican	-87	-13
Puerto Rican	-78	-56
Other	-62	-42

TABLE A3
Racial Integration as Described by Black Students
(Percent)

	Public	Catholic
Few blacks	29	30
Half blacks	28	21
Most blacks	24	32
All blacks	19	17
Total	100%	100%

CATHOLIC SCHOOLS AND RACIAL INTEGRATION

A number of critics of earlier drafts of this report objected that we failed to take into account that public school blacks are more likely to be in virtually all-black schools. This is not true. If anything, black young people in Catholic schools are marginally more likely (49 percent) to say that their fellow students are all or mostly black than those in public schools (43 percent) (Table A3).

Academic performance scores do not vary for blacks with racial integration (Table A4) in public schools but do vary for black students in Catholic schools. While black students do better in Catholic schools at all levels of racial integration compared with public school blacks at

TABLE A4
Academic Performance for Blacks by Racial Integration

	Public	Catholic
Few blacks	-83	-01
Half blacks	-78	-39
Most blacks	-72	-47
All blacks	-70	-52

comparable levels, the biggest difference (more than four-fifths of a standard deviation) is found in schools where black students report that only a few of their fellow students are black. Racial integration does not seem to work academically for public school blacks but it does for Catholic school blacks, and precisely in the circumstances described by Coleman in his famous report: a limited number of blacks in a white middle-class environment. The present author derives no social policy conclusions from this finding. It merely must be noted that the racial integration factor does not account for the differences in academic outcomes between Catholic and public schools for black students. When it is put into the analytic model used in this report (after family and student characteristics), it adds only one standardized point to the explanation.